Joe Stahlkuppe

American Pit Bull & Staffordshire Terriers

Everything about Purchase, Care,
Nutrition, Breeding, Behavior, and Training

with 39 Color Photographs

Illustrations by Michele Earle-Bridges

BARRON'S

Acknowledgments

Barron's Educational Series is blessed with some of the most talented people in publishing. These people take the raw ideas, words, and concepts of writers and turn them into polished books. Elaine Will Sparber, this book's editor, has been patient, encouraging, and supportive in transforming the manuscript into a finished product. Sally Strauss, the copy editor of this book, grappled with my grammar and made sense out of my syntax. Barron's venerable senior editor, Don Reis, served as a shepherd and led the rest of us away from difficulties and into a better place. Grace Freedson, acquisitions editor, was the spark that started the rest of the team down the road toward the first book to combine the American Staffordshire terrier and the American pit bull terrier. Dr. Matthew Vriends, an author of dozens of books, has served as a mentor and good friend.

All inquiries should be addressed to:
Barron's Educational Series, Inc.
250 Wireless Boulevard
Hauppauge, New York 11788

International Standard Book No. 0-8120-9200-7

Library of Congress Catalog Card No. 95-14955

Library of Congress Cataloging-in-Publication Data
Stahlkuppe, Joe.
    American pit bull & Staffordshire terriers : everything about purchase, care, nutrition, breeding, behavior, and training / Joe Stahlkuppe ; drawings by Michele Earle-Bridges.
        p.   cm. — (A complete pet owner's manual)
    Includes bibliographical references (p. 110) and index.
    ISBN 0-8120-9200-7
    1. American pit bull terrier. 2. American Staffordshire terrier. I. Title. II. Series.
    SF429.A72S72   1995
    636.7′55—dc20   95-14955
                                                             CIP

PRINTED IN HONG KONG

678   9955   98765

About the Author

Joe Stahlkuppe, a lifelong dog fancier and breeder, writes dog columns for several pet and general interest publications. A former U.S. Army journalist in Vietnam and teacher, he is also the author of Barron's *Irish Setters: A Complete Pet Owner's Manual* and *Great Danes: A Complete Pet Owner's Manual*. He lives with his wife, Cathie, on a small farm in Alabama and looks forward to teaching his first grandchild about dogs.

Photo Credits

Judy Haught: cover, pages 8, 32, 36, inside back cover; Susan Green: inside front cover, page 65, back cover; Liz Van Sickle: pages 5, 49; Jennifer and Vern Cullison: pages 9 top, 9 bottom, 12 top, 12 bottom, 13 bottom, 16 top, 16 bottom, 17, 21, 24, 25, 33, 40 bottom, 48, 61, 84, 97, 100, 108; James B. Thomas: page 13 top; Melissa Graves: pages 20 top, 20 bottom, 29 top, 29 bottom, 40 top, 45, 57, 60; B. Everett Web: pages 28, 52, 56 top, 68.

Important Notes

This pet owner's guide tells the reader how to buy and care for an American pit bull terrier and American Staffordshire terrier. The author and publisher consider it important to point out that the advice given in the book primarily concerns normally developed puppies from a good breeder—that is, dogs of excellent physical and good character.

Anyone who adopts a fully grown dog should be aware that the animal has already formed its basic impression of human beings. The new owner should watch the animal carefully, including its behavior toward humans, and should meet the previous owner. If the dog comes from a shelter, it may be possible to get some information on the dog's background and peculiarities there. Some dogs, as a result of bad experiences with humans, behave in an unnatural manner or may even bite. Only people that have experience with dogs should take in such animals.

Caution is further advised in the association of children with dogs, in meeting with other dogs, and in exercising the dog without a leash.

Even well-behaved and carefully supervised dogs sometimes do damage to someone else's property or cause accidents. It is therefore in the owner's interest to be adequately insured against such eventualities, and we strongly urge all dog owners to purchase a

Contents

Preface 5

APBT/Amstaff Terriers: An Introduction 6
The Real Dog Versus the Perception 6
The Fighting Dog Heritage 6
The APBT/Amstaff's Recent Bad Reputation and How It Happened 6
Identity Crisis: Other Dogs to Share the Blame 7
Human Culprits 8
A Canine Loose Cannon or a Great Pet? 8

The History of the APBT/Amstaff Terrier 10
The Bulldog 10
The Terrier 11
The Bull-and-Terrier Breeds 11
The Dog Fighters and Their Dogs 13
Finding the Right Name 14
The UKC Standard for the American Pit Bull Terrier 15
The AKC Standard for the American Staffordshire Terrier 16

Understanding the APBT/Amstaff Terrier 18
The APBT/Amstaff as a Canine Companion 18
The APBT/Amstaff and Children 19
The APBT/Amstaff and Other Dogs 21
The APBT/Amstaff and Other Pets 22
The APBT/Amstaff and Guests in the Home 22
The APBT/Amstaff and Strangers 23
The APBT/Amstaff in the Neighborhood 23
Understanding Aggression 23

Living with an APBT/Amstaff Terrier 26
APBT/Amstaff Owners Must Always Be in Control 26

The APBT/Amstaff as a Show Dog 26
The APBT/Amstaff as an Obedience Dog 26
The APBT/Amstaff in Schutzhund and Other Work 27
The APBT/Amstaff as a Guard Dog 27
The APBT/Amstaff as a Versatile Canine Athlete 28

Should You Own an APBT/Amstaff Terrier? 30
Basic Dog Owner Responsibilities 30
Additional APBT/Amstaff Owner Responsibilities 30
Should an APBT/Amstaff Be Your First Dog? 30
A Male or a Female? 31
A Puppy or an Older Dog? 31
Pet Quality or Show Quality? 31
An APBT or an Amstaff? 32
Is the APBT/Amstaff Right for You? 32
Are You Right for the APBT/Amstaff? 33
Pluses to Balance the Negatives 34

Considerations Before You Buy an APBT/Amstaff Terrier 35
The Right Attitude 35
What You Should Expect 35
Guarantees 36
How-To: Puppy-Proofing Your Home 38
Selecting the Right Puppy 40
Before You Bring Your Puppy Home 41
Essential Purchases 41
Housing, Inside and Out 42

Caring for Your APBT/Amstaff Terrier 44
Being Responsible to and for Your Pet 44
Keeping Your APBT/Amstaff Out of Bad Spots 44
Exercising Your APBT/Amstaff 45

Grooming Your APBT/Amstaff 45
Traveling with Your Pet 46
If Your Dog Doesn't Go with You 48

Bringing Your APBT/Amstaff Terrier Home 50
First Things First 50
Socialization Is Essential 50
Adjustment Time 51
The Cage/Crate/Carrier 52
Helping Your APBT/Amstaff Pup Settle In 54
The Crucial Early Lessons 55
Keeping Your APBT/Amstaff Close to You 55

Feeding Your APBT/Amstaff Terrier 57
Balance—the Basis of Proper Nutrition 57
The Importance of Quality and Consistency in Feeding 57
The Building Blocks of a Good Diet 58
Feeding APBT/Amstaff Puppies (Under Two Years Old) 59
Feeding the Adult APBT/Amstaff (Two to Eight Years Old) 59
Feeding the Older APBT/Amstaff (Over Eight Years Old) 60
Feeding Spayed Females and Neutered Males 60
Fighting Obesity 61
When You Change Dog Foods 61
Different Types of Dog Food 62

Training Your APBT/Amstaff Terrier 64
Train Your Dog or It Will Train You! 64
Special Considerations for APBT/Amstaff Training 64
Pack Behavior and Your APBT/Amstaff 66
Build on the Mother Dog's Training Model 67
How Dog Training Works 67
Housebreaking 68

Paper Training 69
How-To: Helping Your Puppy Become Housebroken 70
Crate Training 72
Basic Training 73
The Essentials of Training Your Puppy 73
The Right Training Equipment 74
The Five Key Commands 75
Obedience Classes to Help You and Your Dog 80

Your APBT/Amstaff Terrier and Medical Care 81
Developing a Wellness Plan for Your Dog 81
Immunizations 82
Other Possible Health Problems 86
Parasites 88
How-To: Helping an Injured Pet 92
Emergency Care for Your APBT/Amstaff 93
Areas Requiring Lifelong Attention 94
Giving Your APBT/ Amstaff Medicine 97
When Your APBT/Amstaff Grows Older 97
Saying Good-bye (Euthanasia) 98

Breeding and Raising APBT/Amstaff Terriers 99
The Decision—to Breed or not to Breed 99
Set Your APBT/Amstaff Breeding Goals High 100
The Dam (Mother Dog) 101
The Sire (Father Dog) 102
When Should You Breed Your APBT/Amstaff Female? 104
Mating 104
Pregnancy 105
Whelping 106
Good Homes for the Puppies 109

Useful Addresses and Literature 110

Index 111

Preface

A clear and simple truth exists about the American pit bull terrier and the American Staffordshire terrier: The good ones are as good as any dog of any breed and there is no reason to own anything other than a good one! A well-bred, well-socialized, well-trained American pit bull terrier/American Staffordshire terrier in the hands of a well-prepared owner can be among the best of dog and human combinations. A poorly bred, poorly socialized, poorly trained dog in the hands of an ill-prepared or neglectful owner can be among the worst combinations.

Some may question why the APBT and the Amstaff have been included in the same book. My answer is clear. They are the same breed with two different names in two principal dog-registering organizations. Their needs and the needs of their owners are almost identical.

There are many Amstaff and APBT people to thank. Jennifer and Vern Cullison, Jean Stinson, Marilyn Brewbaker, Sara Nugent, Melissa Graves, Liz Van Sickle, and many others shared their time and thoughts. Michael Owens and Gary McDonald, two experienced dog men, have long been friends and sources of assistance. I want to thank my wife Cathie for her consistent help and hard work.

This small book is dedicated to two giants in veterinary medicine and in writing. The late Leon F. Whitney, DVM changed the world of dogs (and many other creatures) with his painstaking research and no-holds-barred writing in dozens of books.

The second giant remains the most famous veterinarian in the world: The late James Alfred Wight, writing as James Herriot, gave new meaning to a love of animals and inspired a whole new generation of animal doctors.

Finally, I would be remiss if I didn't express gratitude to the many American pit bull terriers/American Staffordshire terriers that have never been any trouble to their owners and have remained excellent companions for many thousands of people over the years.

Joe Stahlkuppe

This handsome blue-and-white male with cropped ears shows the strength and charisma of the breed.

5

APBT/Amstaff Terriers: An Introduction

The Real Dog Versus the Perception

In the last two decades of this century, no breed of dog has been more maligned and misunderstood than the American pit bull terrier. Just the name of the breed has been enough to send chills down the backs of some fairly knowledgeable dog owners, not to mention the fear that the name "pit bull" brings out in the average person.

Contrast this negative perception with the real American pit bull terrier and the American Kennel Club's version of the APBT, the American Staffordshire terrier, or Amstaff. It is true that this breed was originally bred for fighting. It is true that the APBT/Amstaff is probably pound for pound the most powerful breed of dog ever developed. These powerful dogs also have what is considered the most powerful jaws in the canine world. They also have an incredibly high pain threshold. It is also true that with all this power comes unparalleled canine athleticism. Perhaps the most ironic truth of all is that there are thousands upon thousands of normal, well-adjusted, non-dog-fighting people and families who wouldn't own any dog other than an Amstaff or an American pit bull terrier. These people will tell you that their APBT/Amstaff is a loyal, intelligent, clean, loving pet with an excellent temperament.

The Fighting Dog Heritage

The American pit bull terrier and the Amstaff came about originally as an experiment in dog breeding to produce a fighting dog of speed, power, and exceptional grit or gameness (the ability to withstand pain). The dog breeders accomplished what they sought to do. Depending on which expert you listen to, the bull-and-terrier fighting dogs have been around for well over a hundred years.

The Great Dane was originally a boarhound. The fox terrier was originally bred to go into underground dens to fight with foxes and run them out. The bull mastiff was originally a gamekeeper's dog used to bring down poachers. None of these breeds do these original tasks today. A huge majority of American pit bull terriers and American Staffordshire terriers don't now do what they were originally bred to do either. These dogs have been tarred with the brush of public mistrust that has been based on the actions of a "sport" that was outlawed nearly a century ago. The fact that some diehards continue it still has had an impact on the breed.

The APBT/Amstaff's Recent Bad Reputation and How It Happened

Ironically, even with all the bad publicity, the American pit bull terrier/Amstaff is a very popular dog. With popularity always comes a group of would-be dog breeders who want to cash in. Dogs that should never have been bred, even once, are bred repeatedly regardless of bad temperaments, health problems, or genetic defects. Overbreeding of poor quality dogs will ultimately hurt any breed.

The American pit bull terrier has become popular with some people for all the wrong reasons. The general public heard all the horror stories about this "canine monster" and some people just had to have one. The supply of poorly bred APBT/Amstaffs caught up with the demand for the meanest, toughest dog on the block. The rest became a self-fulfilling prophesy. People who should have never owned a dog were able to get dogs that should never have been bred.

Identity Crisis: Other Dogs to Share the Blame

The American pit bull terrier and the American Staffordshire terrier have been given the blame for many sins. Some of these were, in truth, committed by poorly bred, poorly trained, or poorly owned APBTs or Amstaffs. Other misdeeds credited to the American pit bull terrier have been done by other breeds or by dogs of mixed ancestry. This sword cuts both ways. There have also been dogs of other breeds that have been mistaken for APBTs. A general public and a mass media with "pit bull" on their minds will often see what they expect to see.

There are other breeds that somewhat resemble the American pit bull terrier or the American Staffordshire terrier. Sometimes these dogs are blamed, or should be blamed, for bad actions attributed to pit bulls or Amstaffs. Boxers, American bulldogs, bull terriers (the long-faced "Spuds McKenzie" party dog), and bulldogs (the English sour mugs) have all been mistakenly branded as "pits" at one time or another. Even the more dissimilar Rhodesian Ridgebacks, Labrador retrievers, Chinese shar-peis (the ones with all the wrinkles), and Great Danes have sometimes been misidentified as being APBTs or Amstaffs.

The American pit bull terrier and the American Staffordshire terrier are certainly not the first dogs to bear the brunt of public mistrust or unwarranted media exposure. Many dog breeds have "had their time in the barrel." The German shepherd dog, greatly loved today as an ultimate family pet, search and rescue dog, and guide for the sight impaired, was once the victim of bad press when unknowing people thought of the breed as the "German police dog."

The real qualities of the real APBT/Amstaff will cause these dogs to weather the negative publicity and public opinion storm. Concerned breeders have begun what amounts to a canine reclamation project. They have joined together to demonstrate the working abilities of these unique animals, their good dispositions when properly schooled, their great versatility, and their bright and funny personalities. The friends of the American pit bull terrier and the American Staffordshire terrier are doing much to offset the years of exploitation that brought these dogs into a bad light.

Other breeds are sometimes mistaken for the APBT/Amstaff (which is in the very center). Clockwise from the APBT's left are a bull terrier, boxer, American bulldog, Staffordshire bull terrier, and Boston terrier.

The APBT and Amstaff come in many colors and patterns. This fawn-and-white dog is just one example.

Human Culprits

The American pit bull terrier did not get a bad reputation all by itself. There have been quite a few humans guilty of a variety of misdeeds. The illegal dog fighters have kept the image alive of the American pit bull terrier as a savage killer. The breed-for-greed crowd that will mass-produce poor-quality APBTs/Amstaffs and then sell them to unsuspecting and unprepared members of the public deserves a lot of this guilt. The ignorant or uncaring dog buyer who purchases a dog just to have the "meanest dog on the block" owns a lot of responsibility along with a liberal dose of stupidity.

The irresponsible APBT owner who doesn't have his or her dog trained and under control shares some of the blame. The media members who used "pit bull" when they weren't sure in order to sensationalize a dog bite or attack story should know better. Those in the general public who have passed judgment on an entire breed based on what was heard about a few dogs are as guilty as the rest!

A Canine Loose Cannon or a Great Pet?

Is the American pit bull terrier/American Staffordshire terrier a breed that is out of control? Are all APBT/Amstaffs problems just waiting to happen? The answer to these questions is a general "No," but a specific "Could be." There are some American pit bull terriers that are out of control and dangerous, just as there are dogs of other breeds that are out of control or dangerous. To say that about all or even most APBT/Amstaffs is certainly not true.

The right APBT/Amstaff chosen from a well-bred litter from parentage with good temperament, if given good training and good ownership, won't be any more of a problem than almost any other breed and probably less than many of them! If the American pit bull terrier or American Staffordshire terrier were coming on the scene right now for the first time, perceptions would be vastly different! There would be no fighting dog history or stigma and the breed would not have been hurt by overbreeding of poor quality dogs. If you took a look at the APBT/Amstaff in a nonprejudicial way, as if for the first time, you would see quite an exceptional breed of dog!

The Amstaff/APBT is of medium size. It has a short, easy to groom coat that comes in many attractive colors. The breed is large enough to be a good protection dog, but small enough to fit right in with most families in their homes. Amstaffs and APBTs are usually easy to housebreak and do well in obedience training work. This breed could be said to be protective, but no more aggressive than many other breeds. The breed wouldn't have a great many genetic problems. It would be an attractive, versatile breed with many excellent qualities.

Is the APBT a loose canine cannon or an excellent all-around pet? That will depend largely on the dog's owner. If an owner takes time to find the right dog, socializes it, carefully trains it, and provides for it in a responsible way, the odds are greatly in the favor of the Amstaff/American pit bull terrier being a superb pet. With the wrong owner, the American Staffordshire terrier or APBT could be among the worst dogs to own. The irresponsible APBT/Amstaff owner could have a dog that could be as bad as any other breed of large or strong, potentially aggressive dogs in a similarly undisciplined situation!

This young brindle female has uncropped ears and a calm disposition.

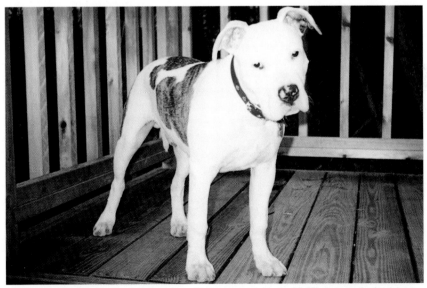

This uncropped dog has a lot of white, which is acceptable in APBTs but not in American Staffordshire terriers.

The History of the APBT/Amstaff Terrier

The American pit bull terrier and the American Staffordshire terrier along with the Staffordshire bull terrier and the white and colored varieties of the (long-faced) bull terrier all share much the same genetic heritage. Whether or not modern breeders want to acknowledge it, this common heritage is deeply rooted in what has been called "the blood sports." The APBT, the Amstaff, and the others all spring from a canine ancestry that fought other animals: bulls, bears, other dogs, and even lions!

To refuse to face the historical truth, as distasteful and barbaric as it may be, is to fail to grasp the source of many of the qualities that have caused these breeds not only to endure, but to flourish. To understand the positive things about the modern dogs, one must understand the negative things that caused them.

The original British bulldog was bred for bear-baiting and other "blood sports." This early bulldog greatly resembled today's American pit bull terrier or American Staffordshire terrier.

The Bulldog

The bulldog part of the APBT and Amstaff equation was *not* the squat, lumbering, quite short-faced bulldog of today. The bulldog of several centuries ago was an agile, muscular dog of medium size, quite capable of participating in the bull-baiting and bear-baiting events of the time. Bulldogs were admired for their tenacity, their physical courage (called "gameness"), and their tolerance of pain—all good attributes for dogs battling foes many times their size.

Artists' renderings of the bulldog of the eighteenth and nineteenth centuries show an animal strikingly similar to the American Staffordshire terrier and the American pit bull terrier of today. This similarity of appearance has led many "fighting pit bull" authorities to claim that the modern APBTs have *no* terrier blood at all! In books and descriptions by some of these authorities, the American pit bull terrier is often simply referred to as a bulldog. These sources sometimes put forth the belief that the American pit bull terrier is, in reality, merely the original bulldog of the British Isles!

Other historical records don't support this claim. There are numerous references citing intentional crosses being made between bulldogs and terriers. The reason for this mixing of two varieties was to increase the speed and activity levels of the bulldog by genetically adding attributes of the agile and active hunting terriers of the time.

The early British bulldogs were not crossbred exclusively with terriers. So admired was the physical toughness of the bulldog that a famous bulldog cross was made with racing greyhounds in an attempt to instill toughness in a very dissimilar breed. Another mixing of bulldog lines led to a new breed. In an attempt to develop a more suitable patrol dog for English gamekeepers, the early bulldog was bred to the huge English mastiff with the result becoming the bull mastiff, a tough, agile, quick dog of still considerable size.

Bull and bear fighting in England was outlawed by the Humane Acts of Parliament in 1835. Dog fighting, while not new, became more popular, partly because of the edict against the larger animal fights, and partly because dog fights could be staged in secret much more easily. The bulldog, so ideally suited for bedeviling bulls and bears, was a bit too slow and too methodical for the dog fighters. More speed and flair were needed to bring gambling spectators to the clandestine fights. Hunting terriers of the time not only possessed an inbred desire to fight other animals, but they had grit and courage of their own to bring to the mixture. The crossing of the tenacious bulldog and the aggressive terrier became more and more commonplace as the demand for dogs to fight dogs increased.

The Terrier

Terriers had long been used for hunting and then attacking many types of animals. Fox terriers accompanied foxhound packs to enter dens and kill or drive out the inhabitants. Terriers were also used against badgers, otters, and other creatures. It was in rat killing that terriers excelled. Their speed and apparent desire to kill rats made them useful in a time when rodents were a major blight.

Some sources state that the bull-and-terrier breeds resulted from interbreeding of the now-extinct white English terrier (which resembled in shape and size the Manchester terrier). Other authorities assert that any of several types of the larger hunting terriers were used in crossing with bulldogs. To support this latter position, it has been pointed out that some bull-and-terrier breeds had wiry coats and a variety of colors not found in bulldogs or in the white English terriers.

The Bull-and-Terrier Breeds

The APBT, the Staffordshire bull terrier, and the Amstaff are certainly breeds that fall into the bull-and-terrier classification (the "pure bulldog" crowd notwithstanding). But they are not the only ones that qualify as bull-and-terrier breeds.

Dog breeders had always been willing to "go outside" a particular breed type to gain some attribute or quality. James Hinks was the developer of what would become the immensely popular white bull terrier with its long, Roman-nosed face. Hinks not only used bulldog and white English terrier bloodlines, but reportedly blended in the dalmatian and possibly the Spanish pointer to produce an all-white breed. The early Staffordshire terrier was next crossed into Hinks's all-white breed to produce the colored bull terrier variety. Other than the long, down face, the bull terriers, both white and colored, have a similar physique to that of the APBT and the Amstaff.

The small, dapper Boston terrier, which has been classified by the American Kennel Club in its Non-Sporting Group, is also a bull-and-terrier breed. Although its house pet status is far from the image of the other bulldog/terrier types, the Boston's heritage contains many of

A blue youngster is curious about a cow.

The Staffordshire bull terrier (nick-named the Stafford or Staffybull) is a solid bull-and-terrier breed that almost got lost in the American pit bull and American Staffordshire notoriety. Although only recognized by the Kennel Club of England in 1936 and the American Kennel Club in 1978, the Stafford is thought to be the oldest of the bull-and-terrier breeds. The working class people of Staffordshire, in central England, had long enjoyed the "blood sports" and the area was recognized for its fighting dogs. Many of these fighters found their way from Staffordshire to America where they played a key part in the development of the American pit bull terrier and the American Staffordshire terrier.

Today's Staffybull is shorter and smaller than either the Amstaff or the APBT. Its ears are always left uncropped (uncut). Currently the most popular terrier in Britain, the Stafford has gained friends the world over for its good disposition, confident style, and devotion to its owners.

the same forebears of the APBT and the Amstaff. The now-extinct white English terrier that played such a key role in the development of so many bull-and-terrier breeds, and other terrier breeds as well, was also a part of the Boston's makeup along with small bulldogs.

Both Amstaffs and APBTs are used to herd cattle and other livestock, as this blue brindle female is doing with this calf.

The Dog Fighters and Their Dogs

Depending on whom you ask, dog fighters are either cruel monsters who have created canine Frankensteins that should be expunged from the dog world *or* dedicated, persecuted sportsmen who have kept alive in their dogs the best of natural abilities to do what the dogs love to do. Either of these positions represents an opposite view that leaves the APBT and (to a lesser but still certain degree) the Amstaff squarely in the middle.

Dog fighting has been illegal for over a hundred years, yet to assume that dog fighting no longer exists would be naive. Even though pit fights still take place, the average person would have great difficulty in finding one. State and federal laws in the United States have forced whatever dog fighting remains to be a secretive, clandestine activity. Even writers whose works contain a lot of information about this illicit activity are probably outside the core group of die-hard dog fighters who still survive.

Like cock fighters, dog fighters were always a clannish crowd whose breeding, conditioning, and training techniques were closely held secrets. It is interesting to note that as repulsive as most people find dog fighting, it was the dog fighters who were among the first to keep careful records about pedigrees. What has become commonplace for all registered, purebred dog breeders today was originally widely practiced many decades ago by the breeders of fighting dogs.

England, Scotland, Ireland, and the United States brought the bull-and-terrier breeds to their ultimate fighting form. Each country had its own variety of fighter. England had its Staffordshire bulls. Scotland produced the Blue Paul (or Blue Poll), a large, usually slaty gray battler. Ireland exported to America many of the small, red-colored, red-eyed, and red-nosed

These two animals are content to be just house dogs.

bull-and-terrier breeds that would become known as the Old Family Red Nose line. The pit bulls and Amstaffs of the United States not only descended from the fighting dogs of the British Isles, but spread the bull-and-terrier dogs over a much larger landscape.

Contrary to popular misconception, the pit fighting dogs are not generally the vicious beasts that are responsible for attacks on humans. A recent news program on television showed a dog fight filmed by a hidden camera. Although gruesome to watch, at the

She may not be actually reading the newspaper, but this Amstaff female has excelled in the show ring and in obedience work.

13

end of set periods of time, the dog handlers were allowed to pick up and administer some rudimentary care to their fighters.

Uncontrollable, vicious dogs would have been impossible to treat in this manner. Anyone who has ever tried to help an injured dog knows the possibility of getting bitten. The dogs in this fight were obviously of the bull-and-terrier sort. They were also in the heat of battle and probably in some pain, but their handlers were not attacked when they took them to their respective corners for a rest.

Additionally, pit dogs are a very valuable commodity to the microsegment of the population that advocates dog fighting. These dogs are not allowed to roam the streets. They are not usually allowed to be indiscriminately bred to the kind of dogs that produce puppies that are readily available to the average person. A person will find a true fighting strain dog for sale in the classified ads of a newspaper just about as often as one would find a true racing greyhound, a true Alaskan Iditarod quality sled dog, or a surefire AKC dog show winner.

Finding the Right Name

Breed names have often been devices of political convenience. The American pit bull terrier has been known as the half-and-half (probably referring to its crossbred heritage), the American bull terrier, the Yankee terrier, and others. As stated, many dog fight proponents referred to and continue to refer to the breed just as a bulldog. The name American pit bull terrier was chosen by an American, C. Z. Bennett, in 1898. Bennett, founder of the United Kennel Club (UKC), not only gave the breed its name, but developed the official rules regulating dog pits and dog fighting. The UKC became the official registry for the American pit bull terrier.

Note: Although the UKC did support and regulate dog fighting in the early 1900s, the current organization strongly disavows any support of any dog fighting activities and will expel any members suspected of even advertising dogs or anything else having to do with fighting. The UKC still is the primary APBT (under that name) registry, but the organization now also maintains records on over 200 other breeds as well!

The American Kennel Club (AKC) repeatedly rejected the American pit bull terrier for admission. The AKC was stringent in its refusal to accept a breed tainted by the word "pit" and the fighting dog sanctioning espoused by the UKC at the time. It was not until the APBT breeders agreed to a word game that the AKC went along and granted recognition *not* to the American pit bull terrier but to the Staffordshire terrier!

There was some support for several names such as the American bull terrier. The white and colored bull terrier breeders (Hinks's creation) rankled at this, and the Staffordshire name was chosen as a compromise. By changing the name of the APBTs they wanted included in the AKC, the breeders of the newly named dogs got official AKC acceptance in 1936.

The name game wasn't over yet. In 1974, the Kennel Club of England's Staffordshire bull terrier was admitted to the American Kennel Club, which already had its version of the APBT, the Staffordshire terrier. To try to prevent any more misunderstanding, the AKC supported one more name change and created the *American* Staffordshire terrier. Both the Amstaff and the Staffybull are well received members of the AKC today.

An interesting "sleight-of-name" opportunity has occurred because the two largest dog registries in the United States recognize the dogs of essentially the same breeds by different names. There are a number of UKC-registered American pit bull terriers that are also AKC-registered American Staffordshire terriers! These double-registered dogs can compete in dog shows or obedience events in *either* organization. Recently a dog with dual registration won top honors in *both* the AKC and the UKC!

There are also APBTs that are registered only with the UKC and Amstaffs that are only in the AKC. These must be shown only within their respective organizations. Their offspring will also be allowed only the registry of their parents. Now a dog that is dual or double-registered must be born to parents that are both double registered.

The American pit bull terrier/American Staffordshire terrier is a medium-sized dog with an impressive physique and demeanor.

The UKC Standard for the American Pit Bull Terrier

Head: The head should be medium length and bricklike in shape. The skull is flat and widest at the ears, with prominent cheeks free from wrinkles.

Muzzle: The muzzle is square, wide, and deep. Well-pronounced jaws should display strength. The upper teeth should meet tightly over the lower teeth, outside in front.

Ears: The ears are cropped or uncropped (not important) and should be set high on the head, free from wrinkles.

Eyes: The round eyes should be set far apart, low down on the skull. Any color is acceptable.

Nose: The nose should have wide open nostrils. Any color is acceptable.

Neck: Muscular and slightly arched, the neck should taper from shoulder to head, free from looseness of skin.

Shoulders: The shoulders should be strong and muscular, with wide sloping shoulder blades.

Back: Short and strong, the back should slightly slope from the withers to the rump. It should be slightly arched at the loins, which should be slightly tucked.

Chest: The chest should be deep, but not too broad, with wide sprung ribs.

Ribs: The close ribs should be well sprung, with deep back ribs.

Tail: Short in comparison to size, the tail should be set low and tapering to a fine point. It should not be carried over the back. A bobbed tail is not acceptable.

Legs: The legs should be large and round boned, with straight, upright pasterns, and reasonably strong. The feet should be of medium size. The gait should be light and springy, with no rolling or pacing.

Thigh: The thigh should be long with muscles developed and hocks down straight.

Coat: The coat should be glossy, and short and stiff to the touch.

Color: Any color or markings are permissible.

Weight: The weight is not important. The preferred weight for females is from 30 to 50 pounds (13.6–22.7 kg); for males, from 35 to 60 pounds (15.9–27.2 kg).

The same dog, a dual-registered APBT/Amstaff, now takes home a ribbon at a UKC event.

The AKC Standard for the American Staffordshire Terrier

General Impression: The American Staffordshire terrier should give the impression of great strength for its size, a well put together dog, muscular, but agile and graceful, keenly alive to its surroundings. It should be stocky, not long-legged or racy in outline. Its courage is proverbial.

Head: The head should be medium length, deep through, with a broad skull, very pronounced cheek muscles, and a distinct stop; and the ears are set high.

Ears: The ears should be cropped or uncropped, the latter preferred. Uncropped ears should be short and held half rose or prick. A full drop is to be penalized.

Eyes: The eyes should be dark and round, laid down in the skull and set far apart. No pink eyelids.

Muzzle: Medium length, the muzzle should be rounded on the upper side to fall away abruptly below the eyes.

The jaws are well defined. The under-jaw is to be strong and have biting power. The lips are close and even, with no looseness. The upper teeth are to meet tightly outside the lower teeth in front. The nose is definitely black.

Neck: The neck should be heavy, slightly arched, tapering from the shoulders to the back of the skull, with no looseness of skin. Medium in length.

Shoulders: The shoulders should be strong and muscular, with blades wide and sloping.

Back: The back should be fairly short and have a slight sloping from the withers to the rump, with a gentle short slope at the rump to the base of the tail. The loins should be slightly tucked.

Body: The body should have well-sprung ribs, deep in the rear. All ribs should be close together. The forelegs should be set rather wide apart to permit chest development. The chest should be deep and round.

Tail: Short in comparison to size, the tail should be low set, tapering to

An American Staffordshire wins a ribbon at an AKC show.

16

This puppy may be in charge of the truck, but he cannot seem to make his ears stay put.

a fine point; not curled or held over the back. Not docked.

Legs: The front legs should be straight, with large or round bones, and pastern upright. There should be no resemblance of a bend in the front. The hindquarters should be well muscled, let down at the hocks, turning neither in nor out. The feet should be of moderate size, well arched, and compact. The gait must be springy without roll or pace.

Coat: The coat should be short, close, stiff to the touch, and glossy.

Color: Any color, solid, parti, or patched is permissible, but all white, more than 80 percent white, black and tan, and liver are not to be encouraged.

Size: The height and weight should be in proportion. A height of about 18 to 19 inches (45.7–48.3 cm) at the shoulders for the male and 17 to 18 inches (43.2–45.7 cm) for the female is to be considered preferable.

Faults: Faults to be penalized are: Dudley nose, light or pink eyes, tail too long or badly carried, undershot or overshot mouth.

Understanding the APBT/Amstaff Terrier

Perhaps no breed of dog has been subjected to as much misunderstanding as the American pit bull terrier. This maligning has spilled over onto the Amstaff, the Staffordshire bull terrier, the bull terrier, and several other breeds. At best, the APBT and kindred breeds are victims of public misapprehension. At worst, these dogs are met with fear and irrational loathing.

The great rise in popularity of pit bulls, rottweilers, and other potentially aggressive "protection" dogs has advanced this mentality by creating a market for such dogs. This has led to over-production of puppies from ill-advised breedings. It has been justified by irresponsible breeders whose goal is not improvement of a breed but exploitation of a breed for profit.

Like any dogs bred for a specific job, the need to do that job is generally still close to the surface. Cocker spaniels from generations of show stock still pay attention to birds and may even point as their ancestors were bred to do. Collies and Shetland sheepdogs still have definite herding instincts. Pet beagles still have the motivation to trail rabbits and other small game. Amstaffs and APBTs were bred originally to fight other dogs. To deny that lingering vestiges of this behavior are not present within some of these dogs would be naive and untrue. To say that all, or even most, American pit bull terriers and American Staffordshire terriers are vicious, dangerous animals is also false.

Like other breeds, the American pit bull terrier and the American Staffordshire terrier will become what their breeding, socialization, training, and care (or lack thereof) allow them to become. For their size, height, and weight, there are no more powerful dogs in the world. Their fighting legacy, their overall musculature can be developed in either a positive or a negative way. The APBT or the Amstaff can be among the best of pets for an aware and responsible dog owner. In the hands of a malevolent, neglectful, or ignorant owner, the same dog could become a canine menace. The breeding, socialization, training, and most of all, the owner of an APBT or an Amstaff, will determine which of these dogs will emerge!

The APBT/Amstaff as a Canine Companion

The American Staffordshire terrier and the American pit bull terrier can be excellent companion dogs for the caring and consistent owner. Dedication to their humans is a breed trait, but sometimes overprotectiveness is too. The wise owner will do everything possible to foster, develop, encourage, and insure the dog's positive traits.

A well-bred, well-trained APBT or Amstaff will be an excellent family dog. Thousands and thousands of people have enjoyed them as pets without any problems. Former presidents, movie stars, and world leaders have owned APBTs or Amstaffs with nothing but good things to say about them. These dogs were family-oriented pets that represented no threat to the neighbors or to the community in general.

The problems attributed to pit bulls have generally been seen in poorly bred and poorly trained animals that had not been adequately socialized to other animals and people. A powerful, active dog (of any breed or mixture of breeds) needs to have an excellent temperament and be thoroughly trained. Without these essentials, trouble awaits.

The APBT or the Amstaff is certainly not the right pet for everyone. A powerful dog will need adequate control. Some older people and children cannot physically supply that control. A first-time dog owner, in the minds of many experienced dog breeders, should *not* buy an APBT or an Amstaff! An insecure person who wants only an aggressive dog to bolster some personal human inadequacy should *never* become an owner of one of these dogs. An uncaring or negligent person should not buy an Amstaff or an APBT (or any other dog for that matter!).

The best candidate for ownership of an American pit bull terrier or an American Staffordshire terrier is someone who has a good understanding of dogs from personal experience. This person is usually willing to seek out just the right dog from the best breeding lines that have a family history of excellent temperaments. This potential dog owner will want to assume the socializing and training responsibilities that will help develop the dog of his or her choice into an excellent canine citizen. This prospective owner will provide good care for the APBT or Amstaff and will insure that the dog has the right food, lodging, veterinary care, and human interaction.

The APBT/Amstaff and Children

The well-bred, well-socialized, well-trained American pit bull terrier is usu-

ally less a threat to children than the children are to it. An overwhelming majority of dog bites in the United States involve dogs other than the APBT, but to some toy breeds, cocker spaniels, and cocker crosses. The number of bites relate directly to the immense popularity and casual breeding backgrounds of many of these dogs.

The *Little Rascals* comedy films of several decades ago featured a dog, Pete or Petey the Pup, of American pit bull terrier/Amstaff breeding. This dog (or several dogs according to one source) was recognized by a circle painted around the dog's left eye. Pete was claimed by both the UKC's American Pit bull terrier contingent *and* the AKC's American Staffordshire (then simply Staffordshire terrier) followers. Petey worked with some of the most popular child actors of the time and in the dizzying climate of a studio back lot. No serious problems from Pete, the American pit bull terrier/American Staffordshire terrier, have ever come to light.

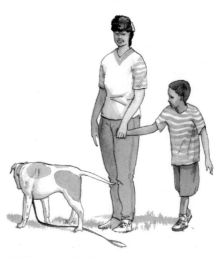

Children should always be taught dog safety, which includes never approaching a strange dog without an adult being present.

These two five year olds are the best of friends.

Many responsible breeders of Amstaffs and APBTs raise their dogs with their children. These knowledgeable dog people train their dogs and their children to understand and appropriately interact with one another. Certainly some Amstaffs and APBTs have bitten humans, some of whom were children, but so have dogs

This bull terrier, APBT/Amstaff, and young boy enjoy watching TV together.

of every breed! Some breeds are overwhelmingly greater potential biters than the APBT/Amstaff.

Teaching Your Children Dog Safety

Children need to be taught how to approach strange dogs of any breed, just as dogs need to be socialized to and with children. Children need to learn correct behavior around dogs; to not attempt to take away a dog's food; not to approach an injured animal; not to act in a way that could be perceived by the dog as threatening. Dogs need good training and need to be in a household where all humans, including children, have a higher ranking in the pack (see Pack Behavior and Your APBT/Amstaff, page 66) than the dogs.

• Children should be taught never to approach a stray dog without a responsible adult being there.

• Children should be taught not to run up to a strange dog, even if the dog is on a leash.

• Children should be taught not to get right in the face of a dog they do not know, and especially not to make direct eye contact with such a dog.

• Children need to learn the right ways to approach a dog so as not to threaten it, that is, quietly and from a nonfrontal direction.

• Children need to speak calmly to a dog and slowly offer a hand for the animal to sniff by way of introduction.

• Children need to learn a dog's "sign language" that says it may not be safe to approach and to never approach a dog showing these signs:

1. Aggression—ruffled hair on its back and neck (to try to be as large as it can be), stiffness, ears and tail erect and not at ease, possible growling, and a generally challenging posture.

2. Frightened—cringing, "ground-hugging," trying to be as small as possible, tail down on the ground or held tightly between its legs, and a generally terrified or suspicious posture.

Note: Dogs exhibiting a combination of aggression and fright are often the most dangerous.

3. Injured—possibly lying down, whimpering, even loudly crying with pain.

4. A dog that is eating and that wants to protect its food.

5. A male dog intent on pursuing or even mating with a female.

6. A mother dog with puppies.

7. Children should be taught not to run away from a dog, as this may encourage a chase.

8. Children should avoid loud or rough playing around a protective dog.

There are many, many children who have grown up with American pit bull terriers and American Staffordshire terriers with nothing but the deepest love for their pets. A well-bred and well-trained APBT or Amstaff can be every bit as good a canine companion for children as any other breed. The key is to search for the well-bred dog and train it properly.

The APBT/Amstaff and Other Dogs

The ancestors of the American pit bull terrier and the American Staffordshire terrier were originally bred to fight other dogs in staged dog fights in pits. Not only did these fights require a powerful canine athlete, they also required dogs that relished such contests. Dogs that are strangers will test the limits of each other, not unlike some school boys on the playground. When an APBT or an Amstaff is confronted by another dog, there is always a possibility of conflict. This is true of all breeds. That an APBT or an Amstaff is involved should only increase the human control factors that should be always present.

Because no dog, not just an Amstaff or an APBT, should be allowed to run about freely in a neighborhood, con-

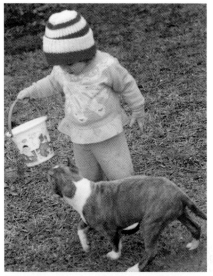

This little girl has a little blue-brindle friend to help her.

tacts between strange dogs should always be under controlled circumstances. During walks on the street or in the park, the APBT or Amstaff should be controlled by the following:

1. A knowledgeable, aware owner who is physically and mentally capable of avoiding obvious troublesome situations.

Children should learn dog sign language to recognize aggressive dogs and frightened dogs. Both could be dangerous.

You should move slowly, allowing a dog that does not know you to sniff your hand before you attempt to pet it.

2. Thorough training that should make the Amstaff or APBT obedient to every command, even when under considerable stress.

3. A sturdy collar and lead (leash) that is securely held by an alert owner.

When describing a particular breed's interaction with strange dogs, dog book writers seem to take some pride in saying things like, "The such-and-such doesn't look for trouble, but is able to take care of itself with other dogs." Such remarks seem to mean whatever breed under discussion will fight if given no other option and will give a good account of itself. That the APBT or the Amstaff would "give a good account of itself" should be taken for granted, but this should *never* be allowed to happen.

A well-known breeder of American Staffordshire and APBTs sold a promising young show and stud dog prospect to a young man with strict advice to avoid physical conflicts with other animals. The man failed to heed the warning and allowed his young male to catch and kill squirrels in a city park. He then allowed it to "roll" (in pit dog language) or briefly fight with a rottweiler in the same park. This male's naturally aggressive tendencies were positively reinforced. Thus encouraged by his owner, this young dog began to be more and more aggressive toward other animals. Ultimately the dog was returned to the breeder who spent months of intense training in an attempt to change the dog's aggressive behavior.

The APBT/Amstaff and Other Pets

A home with other pets needs to take the same wise precautions with Amstaff and APBTs that it would with any other breed. Until an adult dog of any breed understands that other pets belong in the home and are not to be chased or harmed, it must be constantly monitored by humans when in the presence of these other pets.

A puppy being brought into a home with other animals there can be socialized to accept these other pets as part of the living arrangements. An adequately socialized APBT or Amstaff is no more a threat to other pets than would be any other dog with similar socialization and training.

The APBT/Amstaff and Guests in the Home

These dogs have ancestry that were bred to attack other animals, not other humans. In an ironic twist, the pit dog breeders enhanced this animal's aggressive behavior, but would not and could not tolerate fighters with human aggressive tendencies. Although there are some poorly bred APBTs and American Staffordshires that may show aggressive actions toward humans, these must be considered aberrations from the well-bred norm.

Many guests find that the only threat they face from most American pit bull terriers or Amstaff terriers is being "licked to death." These are, by nature, friendly dogs that will shower a friend of the master or mistress with considerable affection. Early in preparation for this book, I was invited to a breeder's home. Seated on a couch, I observed five double-registered APBTs/Amstaffs watching me. The breeder left the room for a telephone call and the dogs approached the couch. First one and then another politely sniffed my shoes and pant legs. Then, as if by signal, they relaxed and went about their regular activities. Two dogs, both females, stayed near me. One lay contentedly at my feet and the other, a large blue and white dog, put her considerable head on my knee for petting.

Normally, a guest in the home will be accepted after being welcomed by a dog's owner. Threatening actions may attract a dog's attention, but a friendly guest should have no cause for apprehension.

Dogs do seem to sense fear in a person and some people have developed what amounts to a phobia about dogs in general and the pit bull specifically. If a guest has such feelings, legitimate or otherwise, perhaps a prudent dog owner should be gracious and put a dog in its kennel, crate, or some other place away from the guest.

The APBT/Amstaff and Strangers

As with guests in the home, a stranger may find APBTs or Amstaffs mainly friendly and curious. Another irony is that these breeds do not make exceptional guard dogs. Albeit that their presence and their reputations make them a considerable deterrent to trespassers, most well-bred, well-trained, well-socialized dogs of these breeds will pose no danger to a mannerly stranger.

The wise dog owner keeps pets under control, thus avoiding accidental confrontations that could lead to trouble. By having a fenced yard or by keeping the APBT/Amstaff inside or in a kennel area, most negative interaction with strangers can be prevented.

The APBT/Amstaff in the Neighborhood

Stories about pit bulls abound and may impact on a pet owner's relationship with the neighborhood. It should go without saying that *no* APBT or Amstaff should be allowed to run loose. This shows a lack of regard for one's neighbors and is probably against the law. Fences, kennels, and leashes all make for good neighbors!

Some communities, states, counties, and even countries have enacted banning legislation against certain breeds of dogs, among them the APBT/Amstaff. These laws are probably nonsensical in most cases because they are often unenforceable and misdirected, but they are in place and should be taken into consideration before purchasing a dog that would fall under such legal restrictions.

The owner of the APBT is like the biology professor whose small child told everyone, "My daddy has a king cobra in our house." This story spread throughout the neighborhood until city officials dispatched two police officers to investigate. Knocking on the door and being admitted by the professor, the police drew their pistols and were confronted by a king snake, not a king cobra, safely ensconced in a large glass-covered aquarium.

The owner of the APBT is like "Caesar's wife" and must go to further extremes to assure the community that his or her dog is a pet not a threat. This may be unjust, unfair, and unrealistic, but in many places it is a fact of life. Being a responsible APBT/Amstaff owner may be more of a task than owning other dogs, but many people have found APBTs and Amstaffs well worth it!

Understanding Aggression

Many terrier breeds were bred to possess gameness or "grit" as it is

Whatever this baby is doing, his canine baby-sitter is paying close attention.

sometimes called. The earth terriers: Scotties, Sealyhams, Jack Russells, and others were known to go into the burrow of animals and fight or drive out the prey. These earth terriers required gameness to do their job. This gameness was often associated with aggressiveness toward other animals.

Animal aggressive behavior was a needed element in these tough, little hunting dogs. Human aggressiveness was not. A terrier that would fight or attack its master was not valued, probably was done away with and certainly was never allowed to reproduce. Animal aggressiveness had its place, aggressiveness toward humans did not.

The very mechanics of the pit, as distasteful as they may be, necessitated that fighting dogs be picked up and handled by their owners during the fight. A dog that would injure its handler was a liability. Pit dogs were required to be ready to fight other dogs, but they could not be man-fight-

ers or they were usually destroyed.

The pit dog people were among the first dog breeders to keep careful records and breed intensely for specific goals. These goals did not include viciousness toward human beings. The vicious label for the pit bull is of quite recent origin. It stems from the current popularity of these breeds.

Popularity has been a curse to *every* breed of dog that has had to endure it. When a breed becomes popular, the greedy and uncaring people who call themselves dog breeders come along to rake in some of the cash to be made from producing pups of this or that breed. Much of this breeding is done without any regard for the quality of the breeding stock or the outcomes of the dogs and humans who buy them.

Most breeds will have their share of dogs that are animal *and* human aggressive. Unscrupulous breeders have capitalized on these aggressive traits by breeding such dogs together

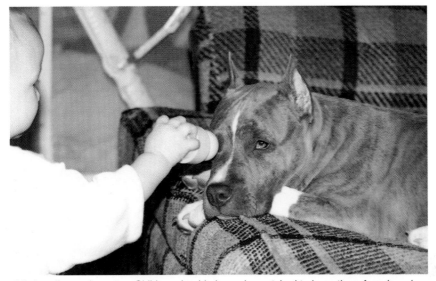

A baby offers a dog a toy. Children should always be watched to keep them from harming a pet.

and producing specimens of breeds that normally do not possess such doubly aggressive temperaments. The American pit bull terrier has been the victim of this kind of breeding. There are some pit bulls that cannot be trusted around people or animals and that should probably be destroyed.

The Amstaff and the APBT from temperamentally sound genetic backgrounds with adequate socialization, adequate training, and caring owners are not the same dogs as the vicious hyper-aggressives that have been turned out by calloused, unthinking, or greedy breeders. The best American Staffordshire and the best American pit bull dog families will produce excellent pet and companion dogs that any knowledgeable dog owner would be proud to own. Don't settle for anything less than the best!

Living with an
APBT/Amstaff Terrier

APBT/Amstaff Owners Must Always Be in Control

When you are the owner of one of the most powerful dogs for its size in the world, you must protect the dog and others around it by maintaining as much control as possible. This control comes from learning as much as possible about the APBT/Amstaff and then applying what you've learned wisely and consistently.

Control can also mean a fully fenced backyard, the right leashes and collars, and good training for you and the dog. Just being aware of possible problems and alert to things going on around you and your dog is a good addition to the other controls you will want in place.

The APBT/Amstaff as a Show Dog

The American pit bull terrier of the United Kennel Club (UKC) and the American Staffordshire terrier of the American Kennel Club (AKC) can provide their owners a lot of enjoyment in the show ring. Both breeds have been quite successful at dog shows, claiming their share of conformation awards.

Both the APBT and the Amstaff have an attractive, muscular physique in a medium-sized package. They come in an almost limitless array of solid colors and solid colors with white markings. Their short, shiny coat is easy to prepare for the show ring. Their ears, either cropped or uncropped, give the dogs a daring expression that also

hints at the fun loving nature so prevalent in these dogs.

Recent popularity has brought more and more APBTs and Amstaffs into their respective registries and into the show ring. That some dual-registered APBTs/Amstaffs can be shown in *both* the UKC and the AKC only heightens the opportunity for showing for such dogs' owners.

The American pit bull terrier and the American Staffordshire terrier both seem quite at home in the show ring and under the critical eye of an experienced dog show judge. Their stamina and grit help APBTs/Amstaffs keep their composure and jaunty style in the show ring.

The APBT/Amstaff as an Obedience Dog

Along with the fun of competition showing, the opportunity exists for an Amstaff or an APBT and its owner to participate in obedience trials. Obedience trials, such as those licensed by the AKC, offer titles of achievement for the dogs and owners willing to put in the training time to learn an increasingly difficult slate of commands.

The AKC titles are Companion Dog (C.D.), Companion Dog Excellent (C.D.X.), and Utility Dog (U.D.) Championships won in the show ring are placed *before* the dog's name such as, Champion Owens' Mikey. Obedience titles in the AKC come *after* the dog's name such as McDonalds' Gary, C.D.X. Knowledgeable dog people have a saying about both show championship titles and obedience titles; they state that "The best dogs have a title at *both* ends!"

Obedience training has an additional payoff for an American Staffordshire or APBT owner and his or her dog. Not only does the dog and owner have a very rewarding opportunity to work hard together toward some of the most respected awards a dog can have, but the dog will be a much better companion with advanced obedience training!

All dogs, and especially all American pit bull terriers and American Staffordshire terriers, must have basic dog training (see Training Your APBT/Amstaff Terrier, page 64). Although some dogs and some owners aren't perfect candidates for obedience trial training, all dogs can benefit from the training, even if titles aren't their owners' goals.

The APBT/Amstaff in Schutzhund and Other Work

Schutzhund means protection work and requires a dog to be trained to protect its owner or handler in a series of staged events. Most people who know anything about Schutzhund training have usually seen a German shepherd, a Doberman, or a rottweiler fending off a heavily padded assailant.

American pit bull terriers also do well in this intense, action-oriented training. Schutzhund work requires a great deal of effort in training and in practice. The goal is not to make the dog more aggressive, but to enhance its working abilities through training and conditioning.

The American Staffordshire and the American pit bull terrier now have an experienced cadre of owner/trainers interested in developing a new vision of these dogs in socially redeeming and working roles. APBTs and Amstaffs have been successfully used in herding livestock, as search and rescue dogs, and as therapy dogs in nursing homes and hospitals.

The APBT/Amstaff as a Guard Dog

Much to the surprise of most people, neither the Amstaff nor the American pit bull terrier is especially suited for guard dog work. The dogs are certainly brave enough, physically strong enough, and game enough, but many APBTs and American Staffordshires simply like people too much!

The Amstaff and the APBT really need a different kind of relationship with humans than that of canine bodyguard. They seem to really relish human companionship and affection. They are not exceptionally noisy, a necessary trait for a guard dog in warning intruders of its presence. The best guard aspect about either the APBT or the Amstaff is the negative public perception. Given the mind-set of the public about pit bulls, only the most foolish of intruders would dare trespass where an APBT or an Amstaff lives!

A secure fence around the backyard is just one control measure an APBT/Amstaff owner should use.

Like all pets, APBTs and Amstaffs should be thoroughly socialized and trained to help them reach their potential as companion animals.

The APBT/Amstaff as a Versatile Canine Athlete

The strength, agility, and athletic musculature of the American pit bull terrier and the American Staffordshire terrier have put them into a number of interesting physical activities. Farmers, ranchers, and hunters have used these dogs to catch and hold semi-wild cattle and hogs. The APBT has become renowned for its weight-pulling capacities in contests where many different kinds of dogs are judged by the measured total weights they can pull when hitched to specially designed carts or wagons.

The Amstaff and the APBT have participated in sled dog races and have done very well. Only their short hair and traditionally northern-breeds-only regulations have kept these dogs from becoming more visible in the sport of dog sledding.

Corporal Dog, an American pit bull terrier, has served as the official canine mascot of the United States Marines Corps. Another dog of similar breed-heritage was the most decorated American war dog in World War I. More recently, an APBT was officially designated a dog hero for repeatedly rescuing people and livestock during the 1993 floods in the Midwest.

Several APBTs or Amstaffs, such as Petey of the *Little Rascals* movies have become accomplished canine actors. Dog trainers familiar with the requirements of dogs on television and in moving pictures state that many Amstaffs and American pit bull terriers are easily trained and seem to have screen presence.

The athletic build and curiosity of the APBT and Amstaff is demonstrated in this impressive brindle-and-white rock climber.

Sturdy fences tend to make good dog owners and safe pets.

Should You Own an APBT/Amstaff Terrier?

Basic Dog Owner Responsibilities

Every owner of any breed or type of dog should be responsible, aware, and caring. The need for proper housing, medical care, food, training, and socialization are just some of the basic requirements that should be understood before any person undertakes to own any dog.

Unless a potential dog owner is willing and able to give these essentials, dog ownership should be delayed or even avoided altogether. To own a pet and to not provide for its needs is certainly cruel, neglectful, and even illegal.

Additional APBT/Amstaff Owner Responsibilities

Because of controversy that surrounds dogs of the APBT and American Staffordshire terrier kind,

A puppy will grow up with you and become what you make of it.

potential owners of these dogs must be even more aware of their responsibilities than owners of many other breeds. The owner of an American pit bull terrier or an Amstaff will need:
• An aware, alert approach to APBT/Amstaff ownership, recognizing the need for the best quality dog from the best quality background.
• An understanding that not everyone will welcome the presence of an Amstaff or an APBT in a neighborhood, a city park, or even on a public street accompanied by its owner!
• Adequate fencing, adequate housing, adequate training, positive attitudes about protecting an APBT or an Amstaff from becoming lost, strayed, or involved in something that could bring harm.
• Previous personal experience with other kinds of dogs combined with a high degree of acquired knowledge about Amstaffs and APBTs.
• An understanding and protective attitude by all members of an APBT's or an Amstaff's household that the pet's control and safety should always be a prime consideration!

Should an APBT/Amstaff Be Your First Dog?

It is the opinion of a number of people who know and love these breeds that the APBT/Amstaff should not be a first-time owner's dog. This thinking does not mean that there are not some wonderful Amstaffs or American pit bull terriers that could be great first dogs. It is the other way around:

These special dogs need special owners and not every first-time dog owner is special enough.

The physical attributes of these breeds and the negative public attitude that sometimes follows them may be more than a novice dog owner will be able to handle. The well-bred, well-trained, and well-cared for APBT or American Staffordshire in the hands of the well-prepared owner can be the equal of any other breed, but the emphasis has to be on the well-prepared owner.

A Male or a Female?

In some breeds, the gender of the pet is a relatively minor concern. In the hands of an experienced dog owner thoroughly familiar with the Amstaff or the American pit bull terrier, whether a pet is a male or a female is probably purely a matter of personal preference. For a first-time Amstaff or APBT owner, many breeders recommend a female.

A female of any breed is generally a little less challenging for pet owners. Male dogs of most breeds tend to be more aggressive, not that females can't be. Unneutered males will arduously pursue females in heat. In a neighborhood, this could lead to several kinds of negative consequences.

Discuss your personal preferences with several knowledgeable American Staffordshire terrier or American pit bull terrier breeders. Get them to assess your current situation as a potential dog owner. Weigh their advice along with what you believe is a wise course of action in gender selection and combine this with the choice that makes the most common sense.

A Puppy or an Older Dog?

There may very well be some very excellent adult dogs available to you. If you have the dog owner experience and capacity to help an older Amstaff or APBT adjust to a new home and family, you perhaps could consider this option. But, as with a preference for males or females, a number of breeders suggest that if you have never owned an Amstaff or an American pit bull terrier before, a puppy is the better choice.

An American pit bull terrier or an American Staffordshire terrier puppy will give you ample opportunity to mold it and shape it into the best pet its genetic makeup will allow it to be. Unlike an adult, this youngster will not have a lengthy past history (positive or negative) to forget. You can concentrate on initial training and socialization rather than on retraining and resocialization.

An American Staffordshire or American pit bull terrier puppy will have an opportunity to grow up as one of the family. When a family is well-prepared for the addition of a puppy, the youngster can easily become an integral part of everyday activity. When a puppy is brought into an unprepared or ill-prepared household, the chances for a less than satisfactory outcome are greatly increased.

Pet Quality or Show Quality?

The accent in any breed of dogs should always be on quality of the animal's health and temperament first, then on show or pet considerations. Your goals for your Amstaff or APBT will play an important role in whether you want a potential show dog or can settle for a top-dispositioned, healthy animal with some minor cosmetic flaw that stops a conformation dog show career.

There are many opportunities available to show both American pit bull terriers and American Staffordshire terriers. The people involved in dog showing generally greatly enjoy it. This may or may not be the activity of choice for you and your dog, but dog shows are often a good place to start in gaining breed knowledge. Dog shows and obedience events can

Puppies are cute, but they are also very malleable. They will become what they are bred, socialized, and trained to be.

often be the right place to start in getting a list of breeders from whom a puppy could be purchased.

An APBT or an Amstaff?

Whether to own an American Staffordshire terrier or an American pit bull terrier is purely a matter of personal choice. Many top breeders of these dogs consider them the same breed with the main distinction being that of registries, not dogs. In the past, the pit part of the APBT name was enough to discourage some people from owning one. Some of these people turned to the American Staffordshire, which had been bred along AKC exhibition lines. You can find an Amstaff breeder (or an APBT

breeder) near you by contacting the national clubs (see Useful Addresses and Literature, page 110).

Although the Amstaff is still a good choice, the American pit bull terrier of the UKC now also has a bright future in the show ring as more and more UKC (and other organizations accepting the APBT) shows are held. Although not everyone is interested in dog shows and dog showing, show breeders are often the source for some top-quality pet pups.

Of course, there are still a large number of dual or double-registered Amstaffs/APBTs available that can compete in either UKC or AKC shows! Dogs of legitimate double-registered status are neither better nor worse than their single-registered kin, but they do offer opportunities in both the major kennel clubs.

Regardless of which breed you choose, there are some important things that will need to be given careful consideration by you and your family. Of course, any dog will need and deserve good care, affection, and the attention of a knowledgeable owner.

Is the APBT/Amstaff Right for You?

There are some key points to consider about owning an American pit bull terrier or an American Staffordshire terrier.
• These breeds have been shrouded by a lot of misinformation and controversy.
• Not everyone in your neighborhood, in your circle of friends, in a city park, or even on a public street will welcome your ownership of one of these dogs.
• Some communities have placed breed-specific restrictions against dogs like the APBT and the Amstaff.
• Some insurance companies will not issue homeowners policies for the owners of dogs of certain breeds.
• Dogs of these two breeds should have stronger fencing, housing,

training, and other controls than dogs of some other breeds.

• American pit bull terriers come from aggressive ancestry and will require significantly more owner attention involving effective training and socialization.

• Pound for pound, these dogs are the strongest canines in the world. Their jaws are so incredibly strong that some chew toys sufficient for almost every other breed are woefully insufficient for the APBT and the Amstaff.

• Amstaffs and American pit bull terriers tend to be smart, alert dogs that will need early, consistent training.

• These breeds have been exploited for generations by people whose idea of dog ownership differs radically from most pet owners. APBTs and Amstaff have unfortunately become popular with street toughs and with some unsavory elements in society.

• The popularity and name recognition afforded these breeds has caused a great deal of ill-advised breeding that has become a self-fulfilling prophecy.

• In the hands of the right owners, the right American Staffordshire terrier or the right American pit bull terrier can be a family pet of legendary proportions, the kind that you tell your grandchildren about!

• In the hands of the wrong owners, the wrong American Staffordshire terrier or the wrong American pit bull terrier can become at best an unfortunate mistake, at worst a serious mistake that will negatively impact on the owners and the dog.

• Because these breeds stem from dogs of pit fighting infamy, even a slight nip or a scratch from a dog's toenail, can result in legal action and/or legal consequences that probably wouldn't happen if the nipper or scratcher were some other breed.

• The APBT and the Amstaff will need close human interaction, living with the

The Amstaff and APBT have the strongest jaws of all canines. They need super-strong toys and a lot of chewing exercise.

family, being a part of the family to reach its ultimate potential as a pet and companion.

• These dogs cannot be tied to a tree or simply left in a kennel or backyard. They are true lovers of people and will suffer if deprived of lots of human contact.

Are You Right for the APBT/Amstaff?

Before you go out and get an American pit bull terrier or an American Staffordshire terrier, you should ask yourself the following questions and then answer them honestly:

• Do you want an APBT/Amstaff just to have the reputation for owning "meanest dog on the block?"

• Have you owned other kinds of dogs that will give you some reference point and some experience for owning an APBT or an Amstaff?

• Are you willing to invest the time and money to search and find just the right pet for you and your family?

• Do you have the resources and the inclination to help a young puppy get the socialization, care, and training it will need to grow into the best possible pet?

• Do you and your family have the time and space to share with a dog that will need a lot of affection, direction, and attention?

• Are you aware of the negative publicity that has attached itself to these dogs and are you ready to deal with any negative spillover that may affect you when you own an Amstaff or an APBT?

• Are you willing to go the extra dog-owner mile for a dog that may need more than other dogs do, but would willingly die for its family?

• Are you willing to spay or neuter an obvious pet specimen?

• Will you do everything within your power to keep any dog that you own from becoming a public nuisance, a threat to itself or others, or one of the millions of animal shelter dogs that are euthanized each year?

These are tough questions that any serious, prospective APBT or Amstaff owner should be able to answer. If you or your family stumble over some of these, or if an answer doesn't seem to serve the best interests of the potential pet, your path is clearer than you may think. There are several options for potential pet owners who have trouble with these questions:

1. Consider another kind of dog. The APBT/Amstaff may not be right for you and your lifestyle.

2. Don't get any dog at all. Pet ownership requires a great deal of responsibility, regardless of what breed you choose.

3. Postpone getting a dog until you are better able to afford the time,

money, and other expenditures that an APBT/Amstaff will require.

4. Find a responsible American pit bull terrier or American Staffordshire terrier breeder to visit, to spend time with, and to question.

Pluses to Balance the Negatives

Having to consider these negatives and review your own dog-owning motivation may seem to cast American Staffordshires and American pit bull terriers in a bad light. It would be easy to say that one of these dogs just isn't worth the extra effort, but that would not be true.

The best dog-owning family in the world who buys a puppy on impulse, a puppy that comes from poorly bred stock with behavioral and health problems, will almost certainly come to regret it. The best American pit bull terrier or Amstaff puppy in the world coming into a neglectful, careless, ill-prepared family is a recipe for trouble.

Owners of these dogs tell wonderful stories that would do any breed proud. These stories are not only of the incredible bravery and devotion one would naturally expect of such dogs. Some accounts point out their sensitive nature. Others show a brightness that would make the fictional Lassie envious. Still further stories illustrate the whimsical, funny aspects of these powerful animals.

The American pit bull terrier and the American Staffordshire have been vigorously vilified. Even after all the bad press, these dogs have thousands upon thousands of fans who know the actual and the potential of the APBT and Amstaff and cherish them!

Considerations Before You Buy an APBT/Amstaff Terrier

The Right Attitude

Before you begin your quest for just the right Amstaff or APBT there is a good mind-set to adopt. It may be true that Michelangelo formed one of his greatest sculptures from a flawed piece of stone, but there was only one Michelangelo. For you to have the best possible outcome with your Amstaff or American pit bull terrier, you should start with the best possible puppy and sculpt and mold it by good socialization, good care, and effective training.

What You Should Expect

Most reputable Amstaff and APBT breeders will be as concerned about whether you should get one of their puppies as you are. This concern, often reflected in a number of questions from the breeder to you, is a good sign that this breeder really cares about finding loving, lifelong homes for all puppies produced.

You should expect to pay a fair price, generally $300 to $500, for a healthy pet prospect from stock with good temperaments. Healthy, good-dispositioned show prospects will cost you more, depending on breeder and location. Beware of bargains, with Amstaffs and APBTs you positively cannot afford them. Bargain puppies often become much more expensive than many top show dogs would be!

There are perils in popularity. Especially in American pit bull terriers, one can see many classified ads offering puppies in the Sunday newspapers in every major city. It is possible that some of these litters are from healthy dogs with excellent temperaments. It is more likely that most of these ads are reflective of a casual mating of two dogs that should have never been bred. You have a better chance finding buried treasure or striking oil in your backyard than in getting just the puppy you want in this manner.

Remember that this little puppy will grow to be a powerful adult and that you are going to be making not only the puppy, but its adult version a member of your household. Go for the best and ignore the rest!

Before choosing an American Staffordshire or American pit bull terrier from any breeder, you should be certain that the puppy of your choice has several vital documents:

Health records: This will be the pup's medical history showing the dates of all veterinarian examinations, wormings, vaccinations, and any treatments the pup may have had and for what.

The AKC or UKC registration papers: These forms, from their respective kennel clubs, affirm that this Amstaff or American pit bull terrier puppy is a purebred (its mother and father were purebreds and registered also). You should also get applications that you can send to the AKC or UKC (or both if the pup's parents were both

This white-faced puppy will need lots of good care as it grows into adulthood. This includes good medical care, good food, and close interaction with its human family.

dual registered) to register your puppy in your name.

Canine hip dysplasia (CHD) screening: You will want test results pertaining to the parents of your puppy and their examinations for canine hip dysplasia (CHD) (see page 86). Although these results are not a guarantee that your pup will be free from this ailment, CHD screening is the only predictive testing that may be currently available to you. OFA or CHD testing is performed for potential breeders when the stud dog or bitch is two years old.

Note: The Penn hip testing (that can be done only by specially trained veterinary practitioners) and some other forms of prescreening can be done on younger animals. You would be wise to use whatever testing is available to you to ascertain the hip health of your American pit bull terrier or American Staffordshire terrier.

A rule concerning documents: Before you become too attached to a puppy, make sure that the dog's papers are available to you. Quite simply, if they are not available, don't

buy the puppy! Most reputable breeders are honest and are not out to cheat you, but you want to avoid what could be called the "puppy buyer's lament" which is "The breeder said the papers are in the mail!"

Guarantees

All responsible Amstaff and American pit bull terrier breeders will give you a reasonable and written health and temperament guarantee on any puppy you buy from them. This should state that the dog's inherited health and temperament are guaranteed. If an inherited problem occurs, you can return the puppy. Confident breeders who have taken real care in choosing the ancestry of their dogs usually know that a properly handled puppy from their breeding will be healthy and have a good disposition.

You are not the only party in this agreement that will want a guarantee. Responsible dog breeders often ask for several written assurances from you regarding a puppy from their kennel. One of these involves the spaying

The Right Preparation

Before you seriously get down to choosing the right puppy, you should do the following things:
• Read everything available on these breeds.
• Talk with as many reputable Amstaff or APBT breeders as possible.
• Visit a number of dog shows, obedience events, and kennels to actually see these dogs up close.
• Talk to other dog experts, perhaps local veterinarians, dog trainers, and breeders of other breeds to get their assessment of a particular kennel or of these breeds in general.
• Look at your current life situation as to how it would fit the needs of a fast-growing, inquisitive new puppy.
• With tact, review your insurance policies and coverage. (One top Amstaff breeder suggests that you quietly increase your homeowners insurance to the $300,000 level and that this must be done *prior* to purchasing a puppy.)
• Check the laws within your township, parish, county, or city to see if there are any breed-specific laws banning certain dogs.
• Decide on exactly what you think you want, an Amstaff or an APBT (or both in a double-registered animal), a male or a female, a puppy or an older dog, a purely pet prospect or a show/pet prospect. You can discuss color preferences and other more cosmetic aspects while remembering that good health and a good disposition are the key elements that you really want.
• Seek a mentor or several mentors who are experienced APBT or Amstaff breeders who will not only help you with your search for the right pet, but will be around to share advice and assistance as you and your puppy grow up together.

or neutering of a pet-quality dog or puppy. This is done to insure that only the very best specimens are slated for the breeding pen. A spay/neuter agreement does not imply that your puppy is not a good, healthy animal. It only means that the cosmetic flaw that keeps it from being a show dog should also keep it from being a breeding dog. The only exception to the documents rule is that some breeders will hold registration papers until they receive proof that a veterinarian has spayed or neutered a pet puppy.

Some breeders who sell show quality puppies will want a guarantee from you that the show prospect will be shown and given a chance to go as far toward a conformation championship as possible.

Many reputable breeders have a return policy where they will want your

Visit dog shows and obedience events, and talk to as many experienced APBT/Amstaff breeders as possible, before you select a puppy.

37

HOW-TO:
Puppy-Proofing Your Home

Making your home and area safe for your new APBT or Amstaff puppy is a little different than it would be for a puppy of most other breeds. The jaws of even a puppy of these breeds are very, very strong. Things that would only get a little gnawing from a puppy of another breed will practically disintegrate when chewed by a little APBT or American Staffordshire. You may have raised other pups, but this one is different.

You will want to decide just where the pup will be allowed to go. Not every part of any home is a good place for a curiosity-filled little terrier. Talk with your breeder/mentor about additional places that should be off-limits for a new puppy and why. Here are some ways to accomplish this very important task:

• Get down to the puppy's level and look for things or situations where a little dog could get hurt. This is a great, fun, and instruc-

When puppy-proofing your home, get down to the puppy's level to look for possible dangers.

tive chore where children could help!

• Look for electrical cords, low-sitting houseplants, doorstops, and other everyday items that might cause harm to a chewing puppy.

• Reposition any heavy items that could be pulled over onto a pup.

• Make a diligent search (perhaps with the children again) for

Puppy-proofing includes protecting a teething puppy from almost certain death by chewing electrical cords.

foreign objects that could be swallowed by a puppy. These could include thumbtacks, pins, pencils, coins, beads, and so forth. This search is especially important in carpeted areas.

• Check your home for any exposed woodwork, especially in older homes that could have lead-based paint that could poison a gnawing puppy.

• Be certain that your puppy isn't exposed to areas, furniture, or carpeting that have been treated with chemicals, pesticides, or possibly toxic sprays. This certainly includes any places where poisons may have been placed (and possibly forgotten) for rats, mice, roaches, or ants.

• Block off balconies, stairwells, and porches where a puppy could fall and be injured or killed.

• Close off any places behind televisions, upright pianos, or other heavy furniture where a youngster could get trapped. This includes railings or banisters where a puppy's head might get stuck.

• Puppy-proofing also includes thorough training of the entire family about what should and should not be done when the puppy is around. Care should be taken to prevent a pup from rushing out a door and into harm's way. Family members should open doors carefully to avoid crushing a little terrier behind them. No cars should move in a garage or driveway until it is *absolutely* certain the pup is not under the vehicle. Family members should be careful to avoid stepping on the puppy.

• Make appropriate use of your pup's crate (see The Cage/Crate/Carrier, page 42).

• Most puppy-proofing is common sense, but by taking an

When puppy-proofing, pick up any and all items that a curious pup could swallow.

organized approach you will be less likely to miss something that could injure your new family member. Protecting a new puppy shouldn't be an afterthought, it should be an always thought. The youngster is only a few days removed from the safety of its mother and littermates. It has to count on its new family to keep it from harm.

Puppies, like this little brindle, can get into lots of trouble if they are not watched and if their homes are not puppy-proofed.

puppy back if you find you cannot keep it. This strong proprietorial interest in the future of a puppy is one of the best signs that you have chosen a quality breeder. Responsible breeders don't want their puppies to end up chained to the bumper of a wrecked car in a junkyard, given to the mysterious "friend in the country," or sent to almost certain death at an animal shelter.

The little blue puppy cannot yet look out the window the way the big black dog can, but it will not be long!

Selecting the Right Puppy

Suppose that you and your family have decided that you would like to have a female American Staffordshire from parentage that has done well in obedience work. After looking at the rainbow of canine colors that Amstaffs come in, you like the crisp look of black with a white ring around its neck. Your secondary color choice (always a good idea) is slate blue with the white markings, with brindle and white being a third choice. Because you do not anticipate showing or breeding, you have elected to purchase a bright, healthy, sweet-natured pet prospect and will have her spayed when she is old enough.

Because you have taken time to concentrate on the traits you would like to have in your new pet, you have a better chance of avoiding "first puppy syndrome." All Amstaff puppies tend to be adorable and an impulsive person or family can undo all the long hours of study and research by falling in love with the first puppy or with the first litter they see. That first pup may indeed be the best for you, but it will still be the best after you have looked at as many puppies as possible.

When you have found an Amstaff litter that has the prerequisite obedience work heritage that you want and has several female pet-quality puppies with white collars, you should now see which puppy seems well adjusted within the litter. You may not want the most aggressive, but neither will you want the shrinking violet that avoids your touch.

A good breeder will have already begun the crucial socialization process with this litter. The puppies should be at ease and even curious and happy to see strangers. Their mother should be alert but not threatened by your presence, and if you can see the puppies' sire (father), approach, and pet him, you may be about to buy a puppy.

Before You Bring
Your Puppy Home

Well before the time that you enter your home with your new Amstaff or American pit bull terrier puppy, there are many things you must do to get ready. Because your puppy will need to live in the house with you, you will need to make the home safe for the inquisitive, chewing youngster. You will need to work out your house-breaking plan. You will need to make some necessary purchases. You will want to assess each area to which the puppy will have access for things that might harm the youngster.

Essential Purchases

The first essential purchase and one of the most important is to buy some of exactly the same food the breeder has been feeding your new puppy, unless the breeder has been having trouble with this particular food. You can change diets, if you absolutely must, at some later date. Don't change food on a new puppy. It can only add to the trauma the young-ster is already experiencing!

Because your Amstaff or APBT should probably live indoors with you, the next purchase that is also of great-est importance is a dog cage/crate/car-rier which will serve as your pup's home within your home. (See Crate Training, page 72).

Your new family member will need its own water and food bowls. Remember the powerful jaws of these dogs and get dishes made of strong metal or ceramic material. Get a sturdy, flat-bottomed design that is large enough for permanent use and that will not be easily tipped over.

Using your breeder/mentor's experi-ence, get a leash (also called a lead) with an appropriately sized collar for your puppy. This will be the pup's reg-ular collar. Because training begins early with American pit bull terriers

Essential purchases for a new puppy include a crate or carrier, food and water dishes, a grooming brush and comb, a toe-nail clipper, and some really tough toys and treats.

and American Staffordshires, you will also need a training collar.

Ask your breeder friend about the right brush for the pup's short, smooth coat. Like most things with Amstaffs and APBTs, the earlier you start something, the easier it will be. Even though these dogs shed very little and require little grooming, you will want to get the pup accustomed to the brush while it is still very young for those times when brushing is needed.

On the subject of brushes, another essential early purchase is your pup-py's own toothbrush. By initiating teeth cleaning while the puppy is still small, it won't be a problem when the dog is older (and stronger).

Toys for the American Staffordshire terrier and the American pit bull terrier are different from those for almost any other breed. The great jaw strength of these dogs, even as puppies, can reduce even tough-looking chew toys into rubble in a surprisingly short time. Destroying the chew toy is not the key concern. These dogs have a great potential for intestinal blockage

41

because they swallow pieces of what seemed to be indestructible toys. Ask your experienced breed mentor for recommendations about the best chew items for your Amstaff/APBT.

Housing, Inside and Out

With few exceptions, American pit bull terriers and American Staffordshire terriers should live inside your home with you! The pictures that show these tough guys living chained to steel or plastic drums hide the basic truth. Their short coats and unusually thin body fat generally call for housing your pet inside.

So cold sensitive are some APBTs and Amstaffs that one breeder told of her five house dogs (all females) following the rays of the sun as they moved from room to room during the passing of the day. These dogs (all dual registered) would actually jockey

When your dog must be outside, make sure it has a good, warm, draft-proof doghouse.

for the warmest spot when they migrated with the sun!

If outside housing is to be occasionally used in warmer climes or seasons, forget the old drums and logging chains and invest in an insulated and draft-proof doghouse. Such a house should be placed within a secured fenced yard or kennel run.

Certainly the best reason for sharing your home with your new pet is that it desperately needs your companionship and supervision. Human interaction or the lack thereof is responsible for some of the misbehavior that can be legitimately pinned on purebred APBTs or Amstaffs. American pit bull terriers and American Staffordshire terriers need to bond closely and to live with their humans. This can be a very pleasurable experience for both species!

The Cage/Crate/Carrier

Your Amstaff/APBT is, like the wolf and coyote, a denning animal. In the wild, dogs will have a den of some sort most of their lives. This instinctive behavior is just as true of the Yorkshire terrier and the American pit bull terrier. Even if your pet lives inside with you, it needs a place of its own.

There are various models available on the market ranging from the plastic airline-type carriers to cages to crates. Because cages and crates have metal construction, and remembering the jaw power of these breeds, these are the models most suggested.

The cage or crate is not only a humane way to keep your pet where you want it to be at times, it also makes use of the denning instinct. The crate-training concept is also a wonderful aid in housebreaking (see Housebreaking, page 68) and in giving your new pup its first place to sleep.

The Fenced Yard

If you and your family are fortunate enough to live where you can have a

42

Picking Up a Puppy, the Right Way

As simple as it sounds, there are several important things to know about the act of picking up a puppy.

• Amstaff and APBT puppies are often squirmy, active youngsters. Be sure to always support the puppy's rear end with one hand while comfortably cradling its chest with the other hand. This will make the puppy feel secure and keep it from jumping out of your hands.

• If your children are in on the choosing process (as they certainly should be), make sure that they don't squeeze a puppy too tightly and that they follow the two-hands rule to insure safety for the pup.

• Don't try to hold more than one puppy at a time. If you want to compare them, have someone else hold one while you hold the other.

• Pay attention to the mother dog's comfort level. These are her babies and she will want to be sure they are safe. Move slowly and don't pick up a youngster without the breeder's

When picking up a squirming APBT/Amstaff puppy, support the pup's rear end with one hand and hold it comfortably under the chest with the other hand.

permission or when the breeder is not with you.

• Don't pick up all the puppies in a litter. It usually isn't necessary and you don't need to handle the pups that don't fit the description of what you are seeking.

fenced backyard, this will be a real benefit for your APBT/Amstaff puppy. You will be able to give the youngster a longer outside break than you may be able to on walks. Your puppy will be able to run and play with your children with more safety and with more freedom.

There are some factors that are important about fencing for American

pit bull terriers and Amstaffs. These dogs are great climbers and great diggers! They can make short work of flimsy wooden fencing and have been known to stretch lighter gauge fencing fabric.

If you have the option, make your fence strong, high, and tunnel resistant. If you can't do this, don't leave your dog unattended in the backyard!

Caring for Your APBT/Amstaff Terrier

Being Responsible to and for Your Pet

Owning a dog means more than just giving it food and water and an occasional pat on the head. Dogs in general, and APBTs/Amstaffs in particular, need to be an integral and interactive part of their families rather than relegated to the backyard.

Your American pit bull terrier or American Staffordshire terrier will need consistent and responsible care. The animal is an innocent invitee into your home and into your life. Don't make the invitation if you are not seriously willing to follow through on it! The dog can't control the things that happen to it, but you and your family usually can.

Never allow a young pit bull terrier or Amstaff to show aggressive behavior to another dog or a person. Pick up a puppy and get its attention immediately to let it know such aggressiveness will not be tolerated!

Keeping Your APBT/Amstaff Out of Bad Spots

A dog is still a dog, even with all its good points. Dogs, like children, may not always recognize potential danger or situations where they could get in trouble. It will be up to the human part of the dog's family to keep it out of bad spots.

• Begin leash training very early with your APBT/Amstaff. These dogs are very strong pullers. One 60-pound (27.2 kg) dog, in a contest, pulled a load weighing over a ton. Children and smaller adults cannot hope to stop an energetic and enthusiastic APBT or Amstaff by body weight or brute force!

• Don't *ever* let your pet run free in the neighborhood, in the park, at the beach, or anywhere it might encounter another dog or a similar dangerous situation.

• Starting at the earliest age, make it absolutely clear that you will not allow aggressive behavior toward another animal or human.

• Make sure that your backyard fence or kennel fence is strong enough and tall enough to keep an unsupervised pet in.

• When out on walks with your APBT/Amstaff and encountering other dogs (with their owners or without them), be smart and don't let even a minor confrontation with your dog get started. APBTs and Amstaffs are pretty smart and may remember that one time you seemed to encourage aggressive behavior. Consistency is your best training aid!

• Remember that just the presence of your dog may frighten some people. Don't let someone else's fear or overreaction cause your pet to become threatened. One Amstaff owner walks her pet in the early morning and will go a block out of the way to avoid another pet owner with a chow chow that has an uncertain temperament.

• You and your family must protect your pet from bad situations and these include strangers who may want to see what "that bad pit bull will do." Avoiding problems will eliminate possible injuries or possible retraining of your APBT/Amstaff.

The APBT/Amstaff has quite a reputation— as an excellent pet and companion!

Exercising Your APBT/Amstaff

Your pet should get regular daily exercise. This could come in the form of walks with you, romps with the children in the backyard, or in controlled runs (on-leash). You don't have to run a marathon with your APBT/Amstaff because a pet in good condition that is being correctly fed will get by on moderate physical exercise.

Your dog's incredibly strong jaws will need a durable, non-splintering chew toy, perhaps made of hardened rubber or nylon (see Essential Purchases, page 41), to allow it to work off some energy chewing each day. Check with a person experienced with American pit bull terriers or Amstaffs (your mentor, for example) about other forms of exercise or exercise toys that may be advisable.

Grooming Your APBT/Amstaff

As with so many other aspects of APBT/Amstaff ownership, grooming should begin in early puppyhood both as a cosmetic activity and as a part of the youngster's training. Brushing, bathing, teeth cleaning, and nail trimming are all much easier to accom-

plish on a powerful adult dog that had these things introduced to it when it was very young.

Grooming your Amstaff or American pit bull terrier puppy should be done in a serious manner. Choose a place and a time that will be free of distractions, and handle the grooming as an adjunct to the training process. The puppy must be made to understand that this is not playtime, but it can be a pleasant time with you.

Brushing not only helps to keep the skin invigorated by removing dead hair and skin, dirt, and any foreign matter that may have gotten on the dog, but it actually eliminates the need for a lot of baths. Bathing your dog too often will actually do harm to the skin and coat of the Amstaff or the APBT. The skin and hair can become dried out and the natural luster and shine of the coat diminished.

Pay particular attention to the areas around the eyes and ears. These areas can be cleaned with a damp washcloth.

Regular brushing and grooming not only makes it a pleasurable experi-

45

The brush and comb are two of the key ingredients of proper grooming. The other two are starting grooming early and doing it often.

ence for the puppy, but it will give you a good opportunity to discover the presence of any skin problems, minor wounds, or parasites (mites, ticks, and fleas). Your consistent attention to your pet's cleanliness needs will be amply repaid with a more presentable pet and with the additional opportunity for bonding with the animal that a few moments of brushing can bring.

Traveling with Your Pet

Going on trips with an American Staffordshire or an American pit bull terrier is somewhat different than traveling with dogs of other breeds. You need to be constantly aware that there are places where your friendly pet may not be wanted or allowed. Check out the dog law ordinances of any places you plan to visit *before* you take your pet there.

Whereas some locations simply do not lend themselves to taking a pet along, there are other sites that could be excellent for you and your dog. Your primary consideration should always be for the safety, comfort, and needs of the dog.

By Auto

Many dog-related activities, like dog shows and obedience events, involve a good deal of travel by automobile. Good canine car safety is essential if you plan to go places with your pet. There are some important rules to follow whenever your pet rides with you in the family car:

• Keep your pet restrained in some way while traveling in a car. The best way is in a dog carrier of the airline type. When the dog is secure in such a carrier, it will not be apt to be thrown about in the event of an accident, a sharp turn, or a sudden stop. Other restraints like doggy seat-belt harnesses (never human seat belts around the dog or through its collar!) may provide some protection.

• Never let your American pit bull terrier or American Staffordshire terrier ride with its head out of a window. This may look like fun for the dog, but it is dangerous. Insects, road debris, fumes, and other negative things can cause your pet eye injuries or other problems.

• *Under no circumstances* should you ever leave your pet in a parked car. Even with the windows partially down, the inside of a parked car can become like an oven on a day when outside temperatures are 60°F (15.6°C) or higher. Your pet can die in a surprisingly short time under such innocent-appearing conditions. Another reason for not leaving a pet unsupervised in your car is the chance for passersby to taunt or even release or steal it. Not everyone knows that your pet is just out with you for a short trip. All some people will see is a supposedly dangerous dog.

• Don't allow your pet to ride unrestrained in the back of an open pickup truck. This may sound like an unnecessary caution, but many dogs are hurt or killed in just this manner every year. Not only does the pet stand a

chance of being thrown out of the truckbed, but it may see something worthy of investigation and actually jump out.
• When you do travel longer distances with your pet, even with it in a carrier, check with your veterinarian first. It may be best not to take a very young puppy, an oldster, or a dog with some health problems on the trip. Your veterinarian can also advise and provide motion sickness medication if it is deemed necessary.
• Try to schedule travel breaks every hour to give the dog a little time out of the confines of the carrier, a little water, or a chance to relieve itself. Of course, always use a collar and lead when letting your pet out on these breaks.
• When using interstate rest areas, walk your dog only in the designated pet walks. Always be alert to possible dangers in these rest areas: speeding or inattentive drivers, stray dogs, antifreeze or other chemical leaks, broken glass, garbage, and people unfriendly to dogs.
• If your trip requires you to stay overnight while traveling, be certain that you arrange lodging at a hotel or motel that allows well-trained pets. Never try to slip your dog into a hotel where dogs are prohibited; you may be breaking the law!
• Unless you are sure that the food your APBT/Amstaff normally eats is available where you are going, carry enough food with you for the trip.
• Before crossing international boundaries or even some state lines, be certain your Amstaff or American pit pull terrier has all the required shots (with a shot record from your veterinarian to prove it), and possibly a health certificate. Again, because of the controversy surrounding dogs of this type, be certain you aren't putting your pet in bureaucratic danger by going into certain locales where breed-specific laws may be on the books.

When your pet rides with you in an automobile, it will be much safer inside a carrier.

By Plane
Traveling with your pet by airplane is much safer and more comfortable for the dog than it was at one time. Of course all the rules for auto travel apply getting to and from the airport, but there are some airborne safety rules that must be added:
• Before embarking, take your Amstaff or APBT to your veterinarian for a physical and get a health certificate (which is now required by all airlines). This certificate cannot be dated more than ten days prior to your flight date. Discuss with your veterinarian the possible use of canine tranquilizers.
• If the cage/crate/carrier you normally use with your APBT/Amstaff is not an approved airline model, you should arrange to rent one from the airline. Check over the carrier (yours or theirs) to make certain that it is in good shape and that the door and latch work. Other than the conversion kit, which allows a pet to be watered from outside the carrier, don't put any food or water in the carrier.

47

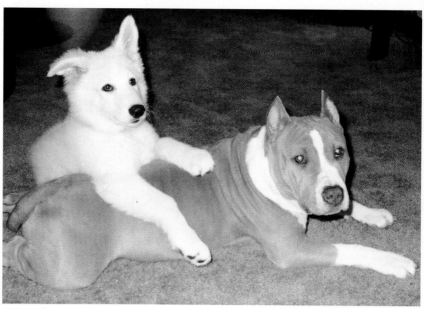

This well-muscled fawn-and-white Amstaff does not seem to mind letting the young white German shepherd have the upper paw in their relationship.

• Prudently arrange your flight as directly as possible to avoid having your dog shifted from plane to plane. Even if you have to drive some distance to a hub airport for a direct flight, it will be preferable. (Some airlines charge quite a bit more if they have to off-load your pet from one flight and then on-load it on another.)
• Always fly on the same flight with your pet. If your Amstaff or APBT gets "bumped" off the flight, get off yourself and arrange for another plane where you can go with your dog. When you make reservations, carefully discuss your travel plans including your dog with the airline personnel. Be sure you understand all that is required of you. Be sure they understand all that you expect of them. Get names and write them down!
• Be early for your flight time; airlines usually require that pet passengers be checked in no later than two

hours before the estimated time of departure.
• Insist on seeing your APBT/Amstaff actually loaded onto the airplane. You can be courteous, but remain quite firm with the airline workers. This is your pet and it matters a great deal to you. To them it may be just another dog they have to transport. Let them know your serious intent for the dog to be safe and comfortable.

If Your Dog Doesn't Go with You

If you have assessed the situation and find that your pet will be better off not going on a trip, there are several options for leaving your pet behind.

Boarding

Boarding your American pit bull terrier or American Staffordshire terrier is often a good alternative to the stress of travel. There are many excellent dog boarding facilities around the United States. Many of these are affiliated with the American Boarding Kennel Association (ABKA) (see Useful Addresses and Literature, page 110). The ABKA maintains strict standards for accreditation of boarding kennels.

Pet Sitters

You may be able to find a professional pet sitter right in your hometown that will enable your dog to stay in its own home. Always use only bonded pet sitters and check references.

Friends or Relatives

You may be able to avail yourself of friends or family members to feed, water, and check on your dog while you are away. Be sure that the person you choose is fond of the dog and vice versa! One alternative is your dog's breeder who might be willing to let an old friend return for a visit.

Your Veterinarian

Your veterinarian should already be a friend of your APBT/Amstaff. The

With his toy held firmly between his feet, this stately blue-and-white male seems almost to pose for this picture.

dog will know the animal doctor and the staff of the clinic. Many veterinarians will board pets for their clients.

Bringing Your APBT/Amstaff Terrier Home

First Things First

The first few weeks and months in the life of your American pit bull terrier or American Staffordshire terrier will set the tone for what kind of dog it will become. The first important steps toward socializing and training your new dog must have been begun before you ever saw it. Initial training is done by the mother, and early socialization should have been started by the breeder. Unless these two things have occurred, the psychological makeup of the resulting puppy may well be incomplete throughout its entire life.

The need for this early socialization underscores the importance of picking the right breeder from whom to obtain a puppy. Responsible breeders know that some human interaction must begin even before the puppy's eyes are open and must continue in a consistent manner on through for much of the youngster's first year.

Socialization Is Essential

Socializing a puppy literally means introducing it to new things and people in a nonthreatening manner. This socialization process makes the difference in whether an animal will be wild or tame and comfortable around humans or afraid of them. All the stories about dogs being born in the wild or wild wolves becoming like lapdogs after meeting just the right human are just stories.

Animals begin to learn early as a part of basic survival. It is generally true that a dog that has not bonded with humans before it is 12 weeks old is not likely to ever do so. When the dog in question is one of the most powerful canine athletes on earth, the matter of socialization takes on even greater significance.

Amstaff or American pit bull terrier puppies are like little learning sponges soaking up information from their earliest sentient moments. Because dogs use their sense of smell even more than their sense of hearing and their hearing more than their sense of sight, the first human scents that come their way will be registered while the pups are still blind sucklings. What they hear, in terms of tones rather than actual words, will become part of their inventory of threatening or nonthreatening stimuli.

The right kind of socialization will introduce the puppies to different types of people: males, females, children, older people, and people from other ethnic groups than the breeder. In this way, the mental and acceptance horizons of a very young puppy are broadened to include many different humans. The puppy learns that humans, as a group, pose no threat. Some breeds become thoroughly socialized more easily than others, but most experts agree that the canine that becomes the best companion or pet is the one that receives the best socialization.

Socialization can also take place between the puppy and other dogs, cats, and other animals that the dog may encounter in its life. Some of the herding or herd protection breeds are exposed to the smells and sounds of sheep very early in the pups' lives, which helps to forge a bond the dog will have its entire life.

The time line for socialization is crucial. Most breeders believe that most bonding with humans must begin early and to a large extent be accomplished within the first six weeks of a puppy's life. Authorities differ on the exact age, but most believe that without appropriate, gentle, thorough socialization, a dog will never reach its potential as a pet or companion.

Early socialization with lots of different people is essential to the development of a well-adjusted APBT/Amstaff puppy.

Adjustment Time

It may be wise, if it is geographically possible, for you and your family to visit the puppy of your choice several times *before* you bring it home. By letting the puppy become familiar with your voices, looks, and scents, it will not be leaving the security of its mother and littermates and going away with total strangers. You might also bring some breeder-approved toy for the pup to become familiar with and then take the toy with you when you go home with the youngster.

It is important to remember that the puppy can certainly be stressed by its being abruptly uprooted from the only world it has ever known. It is important to be gentle with the new puppy to help it get the best possible start in its new home. Even the trip home in a car can be stressful. This is one time that a dog may not need to be in a carrier. Have an adult member of the family securely and safely hold the puppy during the ride. (It may be advisable to have this person wear old clothes and bring some old towels in case of motion sickness or other mishaps.)

Training for your new puppy begins immediately. Some dog experts advise that you already have an outdoor area picked out as a urine and feces relief site. You may be able to "salt" this location with some droppings or litter from the puppy's first home. Immediately upon arriving home, take the puppy to this site and wait until it relieves itself. The smell of urine or droppings should encourage the puppy to do this. When it does, as it generally will, enthusiastically praise the puppy. This first natural activity will be the pup's first success and will begin its training process with you.

Your puppy should arrive at your home when it can be the center of attention and will not be neglected or ignored in any way. This pretty well eliminates Christmas puppies as a good idea unless the puppy is the only gift anyone gets that season. The puppy has no idea where it is and only vague realizations of who you and your family are. It will need a lot of love and consistent care to help lessen the trauma of this time.

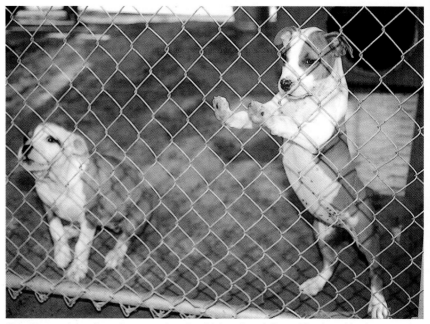

Puppies need a safe and secure place in which to live. A fenced backyard is always a plus for a dog and its owner.

Try, if at all possible, to have a responsible adult home with the puppy for the first several days to a week. Taking several days off from work to help this young, invited guest get off to a great start in your home is time well spent and can shorten this all-important adjustment time in the life of the puppy.

Your APBT or Amstaff puppy will not just automatically know the things you will want it to know any more than a human infant would be able to function without someone to guide and teach it. No one in the pup's new home should be harsh or severe on a pup during this time. The puppy needs to learn its first lessons in its new home in a warm, trusting, and supportive environment.

The Cage/Crate/Carrier

Your American Staffordshire terrier or your American pit bull terrier will always be a better pet and companion

if it remains in close contact with you. If you allow your puppy to live with you, you will discover key things about this little canine that you will probably miss or that won't even manifest themselves if the pup is relegated to a kennel or backyard existence. The pup will also learn things from you by being in close proximity that it will never learn if it becomes "the dog out back."

The greatest aid to allowing your dog to live comfortably under the same roof with you and your family is the cage, crate, or carrier. Utilizing the natural instinct the dog has to be a denning creature will not only be a better way to share living quarters, but it is also better for the dog.

Your purchase of such a den substitute should occur before you bring your Amstaff or APBT puppy home for the first time. After you have given the pup a chance to be a "star" by performing correctly at the pre-set waste relief site, you can bring the youngster inside. After a few minutes of welcoming the puppy home, you can introduce what will become its own place within your household—the cage/crate/carrier.

As with the toy you might have introduced to the puppy before it left its mother and littermates, and the urine-soaked litter or droppings to help your puppy understand the relief area, you may be able to get an old towel or blanket that has the comforting scent of its mother and siblings. This will help make the new den less like solitary confinement for a new puppy.

Everyone in your family must understand that this crate is not a tiny prison. They should know that the puppy will need a place of its own and that its successful integration into the family will go much more smoothly with a crate than without. There is no cruelty or harshness in helping a puppy by letting it have its own crate, and the process of housebreaking is greatly enhanced by working the natural processes relating to den behavior.

Place the crate somewhere that is out of the way but not isolated. Choose a location out of direct sunlight and out of drafts. Pick a spot that will let the puppy see what is going on in the room when it is in the crate, but that doesn't sit right in the main walking area. Your puppy will want to be a part of things, but the den is supposed to be a place to go to rest or just "take time out."

When you first introduce your new APBT or Amstaff to your home, let it have a chance to get acquainted with its new family in its new surroundings. No roughhousing activity with the youngster now, only gentle play. Watch the pup to see if it needs to make a trip back to the relief area. If it does show any sign of wanting to urinate or defecate, quickly and gently pick it up and head to the relief spot. If you make it in time and the pup uses the area, always praise it lavishly. This is the first step in housebreaking your puppy.

Keep playtimes brief with the puppy in the initial days. As it begins to tire, gently move it to the home-scented crate or carrier. You want the pup to associate being tired with going to this place of rest. Simply place the little one in the crate or carrier, shut the door, and walk away.

The cage/crate/carrier is one of the most important purchases you will ever make—for your dog and for yourself!

A puppy must learn that the crate or carrier is where it is supposed to sleep.

There are two aspects of the APBT or the Amstaff that work against each other here. These breeds generally have a lot of endurance, even as puppies. They also are generally very bright. The humans in your household have to show restraint in keeping playtimes brief and not always depend on the puppy for a sign that it is tired. Also, the puppy will learn from your consistent repetition that the crate is the place to go for a rest. Smart terrier puppies will sometimes go to the crate all by themselves for a little nap or just a short break. This association of the den with sleep is a very important lesson for your pup to learn.

Your American Staffordshire or American pit bull terrier puppy will now have to adjust to life without its mother and sisters and brothers. This adjustment is one the puppy and your family must learn together!

Your puppy must learn that the crate is a place for rest and sleep. This is not just important for the breaks it will need during the day, but for night as well! The puppy must recognize that when it is placed in the crate or carrier at night that it should go to sleep.

The lesson for you and your family is that the puppy must be allowed to learn its lesson! The most important rule in this area is that nobody gives in to feeling sorry for the lonely, whining, or crying puppy. If you or someone in your family responds to each whimper and cry that the lonely youngster makes, the lesson will not be lost on the puppy. "If I want them to come to hold or play with me, all I have to do is cry." This is not the lesson you want your pup to learn.

A sad, lonely, crying canine baby is not a happy vision. An even sadder vision is the sad, lonely, crying canine adult that has become neurotic about being left alone at night. Being left in its crate at night will not kill or even harm your puppy. For the thousands of potentially good house pets that have been allowed to become neurotic and bad house pets because someone weakened at the first sound of sadness, death in an animal shelter is a probable result.

Helping Your APBT/Amstaff Pup Settle In

There are many ways to help your APBT or Amstaff settle in with less trauma. You may have already started doing them by providing a toy or blanket with familiar smells on it. You can speak to a lonely, crated puppy sparingly, but with a calm and reassuring tone. This will let the pup know that you aren't far away.

Some breeders recommend some surrogate items for placement in the crate or nearby. You might add an old hot water bottle (that does not leak) to provide warmth. Some people have wind-up alarm clocks that tick loudly and simulate a mother's heartbeat. It has been recommended that a small radio, set on low volume and left near the crate on an all-night talk station might give the puppy some comforting sounds. This might also be true of a tape recorder with a relaxation tape of gentle surf and seashore sounds.

Be certain to put nothing with an electric cord in the crate or in reach of the puppy during the day. Amstaffs and APBTs, even as puppies, have powerful jaws. The hot water bottle may not be a good idea after the first night or so.

As in so many areas of concern with these breeds, consistency in helping a puppy settle in is absolutely essential. If any member of a family gives in to pity for the poor, sad puppy in the crate all by itself, it will undo all the good that crate training can accomplish. Every family member needs to be "on the same page" in trying to help the puppy learn the lessons, however hard they may seem at the time.

Another key area of the settling in process involves what the puppy eats. Unless otherwise recommended by the breeder, you should have obtained some of the same food it was eating at its first home. Shifting foods now can be a serious mistake and should not be undertaken without legitimate reasons. Dietary changes may bring on bowel upsets and even an increase in stress level for the puppy. Diarrhea may come about because of the stress of the move. If it continues for more than a day or two, contact your veterinarian.

The Crucial Early Lessons

You have brought your Amstaff or APBT puppy home. It had a successful first experience (with much accompanying praise) at the relief site. Your family and you made the youngster feel welcome and happy to be in its new home. Each of you was firm in not giving in when the puppy cried the first few nights when it was in its crate. You gave it the same food that it had been eating and its system quickly got over move-related diarrhea. The puppy, in spite of a few little mistakes, is almost completely housebroken.

You now have helped the settling in process take place. Much of what the puppy learns from now on will be additional lessons in good behavior. Consistency is vital here as in every area of pet ownership. These dogs, the American pit bull terrier and the American Staffordshire terrier, are quite intelligent and remember much more than you think they will. If a 15-pound (6.8 kg) puppy is allowed on the couch, the same dog as a 60-pound (27.2 kg) adult will expect to be allowed on the couch. If it is not allowed as an adult to do what it did as a puppy, it will stubbornly remember this as something inconsistent.

Dogs, like most children, are great limit tryers. They will want to see how far they can go this time with an activity that was not clearly stopped last time. A thoughtful and caring American pit bull terrier or Amstaff owner won't subject a dog to these Jekyll and Hyde actions. Simply put, a puppy must be gently, but firmly taught the behaviors that you will expect of it as an adult. A lot of potentially great dogs in many breeds have been almost ruined by inconsistent behavior from their humans. Don't do this to your APBT or American Staffordshire!

Keeping Your APBT/Amstaff Close to You

During the first formative weeks of your relationship with your new puppy, keep the youngster close to you. The crate is an appropriate place to confine a puppy or dog when you can't

Socialization is among the most important things you can do for a puppy, especially a puppy that will grow up to be a powerful American Staffordshire or American pit bull terrier!

supervise it, but it should never become a substitute for the vitally important human interaction the youngster needs. Your puppy will learn a lot by being with you and this will begin the all-important training phase of the young dog's life.

One American pit bull terrier puppy (of an acknowledged pit dog strain or family) was with its new owner, a young woman, when a phone call came telling her that her father had passed away. Understandably, the young woman burst into tears. Still crying, she picked up the curious puppy and hugged and caressed it as she sobbed. She then put the young-ster in its crate while she dressed to go to the hospital where her father had died. The young dog became an excellent adult pet, but each time the phone rang, or tears were shed in its home, it would go to its crate on its own initiative!

Feeding Your APBT/Amstaff Terrier

Balance—the Basis of Proper Nutrition

Your pet must depend on you for many things. Of these things, nothing is more important than a balanced diet. If your APBT/Amstaff's food is deficient in any area, your dog may not be able to reach its full genetic potential. A balanced diet will be scientifically formulated to contain all the key elements a canine needs to survive and thrive; proteins, carbohydrates, fats, vitamins, and minerals. All of these must be in the proper proportions for a particular dog at a particular stage of its life.

The Importance of Quality and Consistency in Feeding

Finding a good-quality dog food that meets the nutritional needs of your American pit bull terrier or American Staffordshire terrier may require some effort on your part. Seek information and valid opinions from several sources. Discuss foods and feeding with your veterinarian. You might also talk to a knowledgeable pet products retailer. Don't leave out experienced APBT/Amstaff breeders in your quest for the right food.

Finding a quality dog food that your pet will enjoy is only part of the search for good nutrition. How you feed your pet is as important as what you feed it. Consistency is a crucial part of a good diet. Continually switching dog food brands will undo all the good of striving for a balanced diet. All dog foods aren't "pretty much the same." All quality foods are different in some aspects. When you find the food that seems to be right for your dog, stick with it unless some problem develops that can be directly traced to the food. Your dog is a creature of habit. When you change foods unnecessarily, you not only unbalance the dog's diet, but you can stress your pet for no good reason.

By feeding a quality, nutritionally balanced product in a consistent manner, you will actually help your dog avoid many food-related problems like diarrhea and a picky appetite. Your pet doesn't really want, nor does its system need, wide variety in its diet.

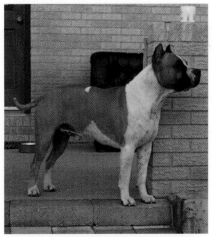

This American Staffordshire is standing watch at its back door. Neither Amstaffs nor APBTs make the best guard dogs because they tend to like people too much.

The Building Blocks of a Good Diet

A balanced canine diet is comprised of several component parts that blend together to insure nutritional completeness. If any of these parts is absent, overdone, or out of kilter, then the entire diet is not doing what you want and what your dog needs. These parts are:

Protein

The first ingredient in the guaranteed analysis (that must be included on all pet food labels) is the percentage of protein. Protein brings to the diet the amino acids that are so important in helping to develop and then maintain your dog's sound bones and healthy musculature. Proteins also aid in the healing and repair of injured bone and muscle.

Protein helps your dog's body in its production of antibodies that fight against infections. Necessary enzymes and hormones that aid the chemical functioning of the dog's body also are provided for by proper levels of protein in a pet's food.

Carbohydrates

Along with fats, the carbohydrates in a dog food formula provide the needed sources of energy to keep the dog functioning at its best. Carbohydrates are usually added to a dog food through some thoroughly cooked grains, vegetable items, or processed starches. Although not as concentrated a source of energy as are fats, carbohydrates are still one of the key building blocks to a successful diet.

Fats

Not only do the fats in your pet's diet provide double the usable energy of the same amount of carbohydrates, fats are also a delivery system for important vitamins. Known as the fat-soluble vitamins, A, D, E, and K are essential to overall good health. Fats are useful in helping maintain a dog's nervous system. Fats also help to promote a healthy skin and a shiny coat.

Another important role that fats play in pet foods does not directly relate to health maintenance, but to palatability. Simply stated, fats make dog foods taste better to dogs. If the food is tasty, the dog is apt to eat it more readily. No matter how good a food may be nutritionally, if a pet won't eat it, all the built-in nutritional quality is wasted.

Vitamins and Minerals

Modern premium dog food manufacturers have done an exceptional job in providing the appropriate levels of vitamins and minerals in pet foods. Both vitamins and minerals like calcium and phosphorus are important in the development and maintenance of a dog's body and bodily functions. As important as both vitamins and minerals are, they can be easily overdone by a well-intended, but ill-informed dog owner. Unless recommended by your veterinarian, leave vitamin and mineral supplementation to the experts. A balanced diet has already enough of both for the health of your pet.

Water

One of the most important building blocks in a good canine nutrition program is pure, fresh water. An active dog of a terrier breed like the Amstaff/APBT will need lots of good water available to it at all times. Water that is hot from the sun, algae laden, or dirty will not be consumed in sufficient quantities to keep your pet in the best of shape. There is no more important job for a dog owner than keeping water bowls clean, away from the heat of the sun or the cold of the winter, and filled with fresh water.

Owner Knowledge

Far too many pet owners consider dog food as an afterthought or minor point in owning a dog. Nothing is further from the truth. The computer phrase, "garbage in, garbage out" is applicable to feeding poor-quality food to a dog that you care about. Not only will the dog not do as well physically, but poor-quality food will generally add to one of the more onerous tasks associated with dog ownership—cleaning up after your dog. One of the things you should know about any food is how digestible it is. Generally the better quality brands will result in less waste in the yard or kennel area. Additionally, dogs will actually eat less of a quality food.

Consistent Feeding

Staying with one food and not participating in continual brand jumping has been emphasized. There are other ways that a dog owner can and should be consistent. Your pet should have a regular feeding schedule. Your dog should have its own food dish and a specific location, either inside or outside, for that dish. Your dog should receive a regular amount of the quality food it likes. Don't double up some days and skimp at other times. Dogs are animals of routine. Feed them on a routine basis to get the most out of the dog food and the dog.

Feeding APBT/Amstaff Puppies (Under Two Years Old)

APBT puppies need a diet that will enable them to grow up strong and healthy. There are a number of quality puppy foods that can give puppies that extra start on life.

Puppy feeding tip: Whatever puppy food your pup was eating when you got it is the puppy food you should probably continue feeding. Unless a problem develops that can be traced directly to this food, *don't change it!*

Consistency is even more important with puppies than it is with adult dogs. Puppies will need to be fed about four times each day at regular times and in regular amounts. As they grow older, puppies can gradually get by on three and then on two feedings per day. Always discuss feeding changes or problems with your veterinarian or with a trusted and knowledgeable APBT/Amstaff friend.

Feeding the Adult APBT/Amstaff (Two to Eight Years Old)

Different families of American pit bull terriers may mature faster than others. It is always important to know as much about the family or strain of APBT to which your dog belongs as you can. An adult dog will not normally need the same level of protein and fat that a growing puppy will need. Continuing to feed a puppy diet could cause an adult dog to gain too much weight. Adult diets need to be formulated for the normal nutritional and maturational needs of adult dogs. If your terrier is used for showing, hunting, breeding, or for any rigorous activity, it may need more nutrition than the average adult diet can supply.

Finding the right food for an adult dog will depend on your quizzing of your APBT friends, your veterinarian, or others knowledgeable about both terriers and about general pet nutrition. Adult dogs can do well on about two feedings per day, but some dogs will need more food per feeding and some less. Any adult canine feeding program must be tailored to fit the needs of the individual dog and not simply based on some broad recommendations for all dogs or even for all American pit bull terriers or American Staffordshire terriers. As with puppies, your dog will do better on a consistent diet of the same food.

A bull terrier puppy plays with an American pit bull terrier/Amstaff.

Feeding the Older APBT/Amstaff (Over Eight Years Old)

Although some dogs are still in their prime at age eight, this is usually a good time line for beginning to observe subtle metabolic changes in a dog. A dog that ate three cups of a particular food per day at four years old may have been considerably more active at that time than it is at age eight. The level of exercise has much to do with the ability of a dog to burn up the energy that its dog food provides. Because fat is one key energy source, it is reasonable to assume that if a dog doesn't use most of the fat in its diet, the fat will stay with the dog. Obesity is one of the greatest killers of dogs, and a fat dog cannot truly be considered a healthy dog.

There are a number of "lite" or "senior" dog foods on the market. Discuss these with your breeder friends and with your veterinarian. The level of average activity of your dog is always a good gauge for the necessity of shifting to an older dog diet. In general, these foods for older dogs tend to move away from fats and more toward carbohydrates as the prime energy source. Although it may take some gradual shifting, largely due to the loss of the main palatizing agent—fat, a change from adult food to senior food can be accomplished in time.

Feeding Spayed Females and Neutered Males

Spaying and neutering is an excellent idea for any American pit bull terrier or Amstaff not to be actually used for breeding. The need to feed these altered animals in a different way is important. As a rule, spays and neuters become more like older dogs in their general metabolism. This pos-

A border collie and a blue-brindle APBT/Amstaff are having a good time in the backyard.

sibly stems from the lower metabolic rate than in nonspayed or non-neutered dogs' lives.

It must not be assumed that a spayed or neutered animal will automatically become obese. As terriers, APBTs and American Staffordshires will be more active than many breeds. It is good for a dog owner that has had a pet "fixed" to monitor the condition of the animal closely and make the necessary dietetic adjustments if the dog begins to put on weight. Usually, good continued exercise and the avoidance of both table scraps and overfeeding is enough to keep most spays and neuters in good shape.

Fighting Obesity

As mentioned, fat dogs aren't really healthy dogs. This is probably even truer for a dog of action and activity. Leaving off all table scraps can cer-

tainly help keep a dog's diet balanced. Making a feeding plan fit the dog rather than the other way around can also help keep obesity away. Plenty of good exercise and never overfeeding will usually do the rest for an American Staffordshire/APBT.

When You Change Dog Foods

There are several opinions as to the best way to change dog foods. One clear area of agreement centers on doing the change as gradually as possible. Rapid shifting will bring on diarrhea and other problems. Any dietary changes should be for valid reasons and not because you liked an advertisement or won a bag of some new food in a raffle. If and when you change, try to blend the new food in with the existing diet.

One way to gradually change a dog's food is to take one month to do it and add in increasing percentages of the new ration in graduated amounts. For example, the first week of the month you feed 75 percent of the old food with 25 percent of the new. The second and third weeks you feed a 50/50 mixture new and old. The final week of the month, you feed 75 percent of the new food and 25 percent of what had been the dog's food. Carefully observe each week for loose stools, food rejection, or other problems. If none exist, by the end of one month, you should be able to feed 100 percent of the new food on a continuous basis.

There are other percentage mixing methods, but this one offers both a very gradual approach with an easy to follow time frame. As with all matters concerning your terrier's diet, take changing it seriously!

Different Types of Dog Food

Canned

Canned or wet dog food is the most palatable form of dog food. It is also the most expensive, the most prone to produce smelly and messy stools, and the most likely to contribute to obesity if overfed. Canned foods are usually quite meaty in their appearance and have a lot of great aromas that dogs seem to relish. If a pet is started exclusively on canned food, it is often quite difficult to shift it to other types of food later. Canned food also is between 75 to 85 percent moisture and can spoil quickly at room temperature. Dogs fed canned food exclusively often have more dental problems than dogs fed on a dry, crunchy food.

On the plus side, canned dog foods have the longest shelf life. They are convenient and require only a can opener to be of use. They can be purchased in one-meal increments or by the case and have less storage problems than one might see in some climates with dry foods.

Canned foods can be fed as a complete diet or, as is more often the case, as a mixer or additive, with dry foods. Most owners of APBTs who feed canned foods probably do so as only part of a diet and in combination with some other type of dog food.

Semimoist

Semimoist foods come in foil or plastic-wrapped packaging and in a great many meaty-looking shapes. They have the convenience and nearly the palatability of canned food without the high moisture levels. Semimoist diets usually have moisture levels around 30 percent. Semimoist dog foods are also somewhat expensive and the stool quality of such foods is not usually as good as with a premium-quality dry food. Some brands of semimoist foods also contain sugar and artificial colorings.

Semimoist dog foods do serve well as mixers with dry food. They also are good travel foods or as occasional treats. Semimoist foods are also good for dogs whose zest for eating is a little off, but an exclusive semimoist diet is, like a totally canned food diet, easy to overdo. Fat dogs are often the result of such feeding.

Dry

Dry dog food is the overwhelming favorite of most breeders of larger dogs. Not only is dry food usually more cost-effective, but it also gives the best digestibility of all the types. Good digestibility not only results in a cleaner kennel or backyard area, but a dog will not have to be fed as much. Feeding less food can help stave off the great enemy—obesity. Dry foods keep well without refrigeration (which isn't true for canned and semimoist foods). Palatability for dry foods isn't as good as with the other types, but premium foods are generally well accepted by dogs that have been given some dry foods from puppyhood on. It is much more difficult to introduce dry foods into the diet of a dog that has only eaten canned or semimoist products or table scraps all its life.

Although no food or treat item should replace regular dental care, dry foods do help reduce film and tartar buildup and exercise a dog's gums. Dry foods have an advantage over canned or semimoist in that they can be perfectly adequate as a complete food source throughout a dog's life. Pups that have been introduced to a good-quality dry food will generally eat it well and do well on it. Because dry foods have a moisture rating of only about 10 percent, plenty of clean, fresh water is essential.

Treats

There are dozens of dog treats on the market. Most of these will be readily eaten by a dog, but only some of them are formulated so that they will not throw off the all-important balance of a dog's diet. When searching for a treat for your APBT, remember that a treat for a dog can be like dessert for a child—it can be overdone. Try to find a treat that will give an APBT a chance to exercise those strong jaws as well as provide something a little different.

Table scraps are not treats and should not be given as such. Human goodies like cookies and candy also have no place as a treat for a dog. Some of these, like chocolate, can actually do a dog real harm as well as unbalancing the pet's diet.

Read the labels on treat items as carefully as you would on a dog food. Try to find a dog biscuit or similar product that seems most closely to match the items found in your APBT's regular food. Use treats on a limited basis only and never overdo it!

Home Cooking

It might seem to be a really caring way of feeding your dog by making its meals with your very own hands. This is not, however, the case. Unless you are a skilled canine nutritionist with years of experience in successfully feeding dogs, home cooking can be just another name for table scraps.

The dog food industry has spent millions upon millions of dollars to perfect their products. The average dog food on the market today will be, in all probability, a much better ration for your American pit bull terrier or your American Staffordshire terrier than your best efforts in the kitchen. Why not turn your efforts to researching which commercial food will be best for your dog and let the experts' experience work for you? Your dog will nearly always do better on a balanced diet formulated by professionals. Unless you are a professional, leave dog food making to them.

Training Your APBT/Amstaff Terrier

Train Your Dog or It Will Train You!

Any dog of any size will need appropriate training. Failure to provide this training will usually result in a poor companion animal. A poor companion animal is a danger to itself or to other creatures—human and animal. Training for the APBT and Amstaff is an important enough consideration to make it an absolute. *Don't own an untrained American Staffordshire terrier or American pit bull terrier!*

I once knew two pet owners who went to great expense to purchase a top-quality puppy of one of the giant breeds. These owners gloried in the beauty of this big youngster, but they were unwilling or unable to commit themselves to train it. The puppy grew into a magnificent 200-pound (90.7 kg) adult that was the ruler of the household. Although he did not come from a strain or family that had evidenced bad temperaments, this big guy became clearly dangerous to be around. He would only do what he wanted to do and would enforce his will with a growl or snarl.

This dog's owners were terrified of him. They could not control him, but were deeply mortified and mystified when a dog training expert actually recommended having the dog euthanized because corrective training seemed impossible. The owners were convinced that the dog was simply "bad" or that they were cheated on their purchase. Neither of these assumptions is true. The owners didn't train the dog and because nature hates a vacuum, the dog trained them!

This sad outcome could have been avoided with good training early on. It is ludicrous to allow what could have been an excellent pet to become a headstrong, untrustworthy danger. Training is as important as any other aspect of pet ownership. To neglect training, especially of a powerful animal like an Amstaff or an APBT, is foolish.

Special Considerations for APBT/Amstaff Training

The popular misconception of the pit bull breeds is that they are not trainable. They are thought by some to be "killer guard dogs and nothing else." Nothing could be further from the truth. The Amstaff/APBT are usually extremely bright, very trainable dogs that really want to please their owners.

Like socialization, training for an American pit bull terrier or an American Staffordshire terrier must come early. There are some breeds where experts suggest training begin at several months of age. Knowledgeable APBT/Amstaff people assert that for their pets, it is weeks and not months!

Because of the dog's strength and personality, many of the things you will want a 60-pound (27.2 kg) adult to know and do must be taught when the APBT/Amstaff is a 15-pound (6.8 kg) puppy. Training can almost not be begun too early. One top Amstaff breeder has her puppies already show ring trained by as early as eight weeks

Dogs are pack animals. Using pack behavior in training your APBT/Amstaff is a smart way to utilize natural instincts to help your pet learn what it needs to know.

of age! These youngsters will obediently walk on-leash, stand still to be evaluated, and allow their teeth and gums to be checked.

Training for these dogs does not have to be quite as repetitive for some other breeds. When it is apparent that the pup understands a command, don't overdo the repetitions. A puppy that becomes bored or jaded with a command will stop paying attention and learning actually stops.

One of the best ways to continue socialization into training is to take the still young puppy out into the world to expose it to sounds, smells, noises, and other stimuli that it will certainly encounter later. One breeder believes in taking a youngster (after it has been immunized) to dog shows, obedience trials, shopping centers, and other very public places. By putting a puppy in these often confusing surroundings while it is still young, the puppy will not be frightened in similar circumstances later.

By safely controlling the pup's introduction to sometimes frightening stimuli, the owner can reassure the young animal and let it know that no harm is coming its way. A puppy given the right exposure and reinforcement while still a young puppy will be easier to train and easier to handle as an adult.

One significant and sometimes controversial method of working with Amstaff or American pit bull terriers involves the area of animal aggression. Many experts in these breeds stress that an aggressive action on the part of a puppy toward another dog simply cannot be tolerated! A fairly common approach to handling this cardinal sin for the pit bull breeds is to snatch up the puppy immediately, really making a strong impression on its young mind. The puppy is abruptly lifted off the ground by the owner and is held eye-to-eye with its master or mistress. A strong tongue-lashing follows and the puppy is made to understand in no uncertain terms that aggressive behavior cannot and will not be allowed. As one Amstaff breeder stated, "You have to make the punishment so unpleasantly memorable to the puppy that it will *never* forget what brought that punishment on!"

There is no reason to ever strike the puppy. The rude pickup, the eye-to-eye challenge, the angry demeanor, and the harsh words should be enough. Many breeders report that one such encounter is all a puppy needs to set in its mental processes that aggression toward other dogs will get it in real trouble with the boss!

This tough and immediate response may seem harsh, but it is in keeping with training methods used by the first and best trainer any dog could have—its mother! Mother dogs are rarely subtle in their reproving of their pups. They do not harm the little ones, but they make it abundantly clear that certain actions will bring immediate, consistent, and appropriate consequences! This mother-to-pup training is an extension of the natural pack behavior that is deeply ingrained in all canines.

Pack Behavior and Your APBT/Amstaff

Your American Staffordshire or APBT will be a loved member of your family. Your family is not your pet's first family affiliation. Your American pit bull terrier or Amstaff is also a pack mem-

ber just like wolves and other canines. The pack is the most important part of a dog's life. It is the natural caste system or "pecking order" that dictates where each and every dog fits in.

Wild dogs will form identical pack hierarchies just like wolves. The pack has a clearly defined rank ordering system with each animal at its own level, dominant over those below it on the ladder, subservient to those above it. The leader, identified as the "alpha" or first male, is usually the biggest, strongest, most keenly intelligent dog in the pack. All other pack members bend to the will of this leader unless they are ready to challenge him for the top spot.

Pack behavior is something that your APBT/Amstaff will usually already understand when it gets to your home. It learned this concept from its mother, and a pack superstructure with its mother, siblings, and the breeder, was already in place. The mother dog is always the leader of her litter-pack, but the siblings work out who is next in line and so forth.

Understanding pack behavior is crucial to training your pet. Like using denning behavior in crate training, pack behavior can be used to make certain that your American pit bull terrier or Amstaff knows its place within your family and is content with the arrangement.

In the dominant giant breed example, serious problems occurred when the pack leadership in a human family was taken over by a dog. It is essential that your pet, of whatever breed, is at the bottom of the ladder with all the humans above it. The giant breed dog in the example was clearly the pack leader in its home and dominated the two human members who lived there. Even if this dog was of a tiny toy breed, this turnabout of the human and canine relationship would be a very serious problem.

Within your home setting and throughout the life of your APBT/Amstaff, you have to be the dominant leader. You have to fill the alpha slot. The other members of your family or household will be the other pack members with the dog fitting in neatly as the last one on the list.

The pack is not some power game everyone plays against the dog. Pack membership for a canine is as natural as any other instinctive behavior. It serves as an important ballast in the dog's life providing the security, appropriate rank placement, and sense of belonging that dogs need. A well-adjusted, well- socialized American pit bull terrier or American Staffordshire terrier needs to understand where it fits in within its social universe. You, or some other responsible human, will have to assume responsibility for seeing that this natural chain of command is instilled in your family and is kept in place.

You can observe pack behavior in any grouping of dogs. Two dogs meet for the first time. They stand rather stiff-legged, often going through the sniffing ritual. Unless a fight is imminent, one dog will recognize that it should be subservient to the other. The subservient dog will assume submissive demeanor and do submissive things to show it is no threat to the dominant animal. Some of these submissive behaviors are cringing, offering no defense, rolling over on its back, or even releasing small amounts of urine.

Build on the Mother Dog's Training Model

Training your American Staffordshire or American pit bull terrier will be considerably quicker and easier if you build on the training the pup's mother has already done. The model for training that she used is an excellent one for you to adapt. Following her exam-ple will make you a better trainer and your APBT/Amstaff a better pet.

Fairness: Each puppy in the litter got equal treatment. No puppy was able to get away with a transgression for which another would be punished. The punishment meted out by the mother was also fair and appropriate for the misdeed.

Immediacy: A wayward puppy was punished immediately while the youngster's short attention span could still associate the misdeed with the subsequent reprimand.

Without anger: The puppies were punished without anger. The mother dog's actions were not designed to injure the pups, but to mold their behavior. She also didn't subject a miscreant pup to long periods of incessant barking to correct its behavior.

Consistency: The puppies were able to learn from the consistent manner in which their mother acted. A transgression did not receive punishment on one occasion and a reward the next time. The youngsters came to understand that certain misdeeds would bring about certain punishments, each and every time.

With love: The puppies were reproved and corrected in a secure and nurturing environment. An earlier misdeed did not force a puppy into exile. The love of the mother and the support of the littermates were not withheld as additional punishment.

A well-adjusted Amstaff or APBT mother will have built a firm foundation for the future training of her offspring. By following her model of fairness, immediate response, absence of anger, and consistency in a loving environment, you will find your pup much easier to train.

How Dog Training Works

The mother's example provides humans with insight into how dog training is actually accomplished.

Amstaffs and APBTs are among the most versatile of canine athletes. They need a lot of exercise everyday.

Dogs learn by having negative actions corrected and having positive actions rewarded and reinforced. If a puppy jumps up on a couch and gets a firm "No" and is gently, but very definitely, removed from that couch, it will soon get the idea that the couch is off-limits. If one member of the family lets the puppy get on the couch, the pup will only become confused and possibly resentful when it is reprimanded and removed.

The keys to training are as simple as the mother dog's model: fairness, immediacy, a lack of anger, consistency, and correction with love. Although there are many schools of thought about dog training ranging from harsh methods using shock collars to quasi-training that really only lets the dog do what it wants to do, the mother's model is one constant that many approaches have at their center.

Housebreaking

Your American pit bull terrier or Amstaff will be a much better pet if it shares your home. For this reason, one of the most important and earliest lessons you will want your puppy to learn is when and where it is appropriate to relieve itself. When the great biological need to urinate or defecate is combined with a puppy's desire to please you, the puppy is undergoing some powerful and often conflicting stresses. You can work with these stresses to assist the pup in becoming housebroken or go against these strong pulls and run the risk of the youngster never becoming the in-house pet it could have become.

Regardless of how much you may want the puppy to become housebroken or how much the puppy will want to please you, puppies physiologically have limited bladder control until they are four to six months old.

A special issue for APBTs or Amstaffs centers on the fact that some female puppies seem to be a little easier to housebreak than their little brothers. Perhaps this is because of the relatively high pain threshold of the Amstaff or APBT, along with the terrier-like focused curiosity of the young males. Many breeders observe that male puppies get so absorbed in playing, exploring, or whatever they're doing that they don't always exhibit the discomfort signs of needing to relieve themselves in time to prevent an accident. In any case, the females are quick studies in the business of becoming housebroken, with their male siblings only a week or two behind them in learning speed.

The housebreaking learning process began when you took the new puppy to the special relief spot and then enthusiastically praised it when it urinated or defecated there. It is important to note that because not all puppies gain bladder control at the same time and because there is the possible difference between males and females, expecting perfection is unwise. If you are consistent and gentle with an APBT or Amstaff puppy of either gender, it will soon learn this important lesson.

The cage/crate/carrier that was crucial in helping your puppy settle in takes on equal importance in the housebreaking process. Because of the innate desire for a puppy not to soil its sleeping place, the crate is the last place the youngster wants to mess up. Crate training (see page 72) will make the task of housebreaking much easier on you and the puppy.

Paper Training

A less effective and certainly less efficient way to housebreak a puppy involves the use of newspapers placed all over the floor in some easy-to-clean room like a spare bathroom or a laundry room. Rather than someone being available to help the youngster make it outside to the relief spot, the puppy is placed in this papered room and left there.

Crate training makes housebreaking so much more easy to accomplish that paper training is almost an unnecessary discussion, but for some people it may be called for. Some lifestyles make it difficult to take a puppy from its crate and hustle it outside to the relief site. Apartment dwellers, for example, may find it difficult to take a pup down several flights to a pre-set location rapidly enough.

Other people find they must leave the puppy alone for several hours or even all day. You could not leave a very young puppy in its crate under such conditions. Paper training is a substitute, but not really an equal substitute to crate training/housebreaking. It will be slower and less attuned to the way the adult dog will need to function, but if used consistently, it does provide an alternative of sorts.

Paper training involves confining the puppy in the papered room. It does not work particularly well with the crate training/timed outside visit method because the puppy will suddenly be given two "right" places to defecate and urinate rather than the one special site. Paper training will require:
• Three distinct areas in the confinement room: 1. a waste elimination area; 2. a food and water area; and 3. a sleeping or rest area where the puppy's crate is located.
• The floor of the waste area should be covered with several layers of spread-out newspapers. Using layers will allow the top sheets to be soiled or wet and then removed. The pup's scent will remain behind on the lower layers and will thus encourage this as the relief place.

HOW-TO:
Helping Your Puppy Become Housebroken

A puppy sniffing and circling is a puppy about to make a mess. Watch for this behavior and hurry the youngster outside.

Crate training will play the role it does in housebreaking when you know when your puppy will most need to void waste or urine, and you will plan trips to the relief area based on this knowledge. After the puppy drinks some water or eats some puppy food, the additional pressure on its bladder or colon will mean a trip outside is needed. Follow these suggestions to help your puppy:

• Take the youngster to the appointed waste place after each meal or drink.
• Plan a trip there after periods of prolonged active play.
• Take the pup out of its crate and go to the relief spot as late at night as possible.

• Take the puppy out as early in the morning as you can.
• Although very late or early trips may become less necessary as the puppy grows up, plan on relief breaks several times a day whenever the dog is in your home.
• Recognize the telltale signs that a puppy or dog may give when an outside trip is needed:
1. A general look of discomfort or anxiety on the dog's face.

2. Circling in one spot as if looking for a clue where to go.
3. A dog that stays near the door going outside.
4. Whining and whimpering and running toward the door to get your attention.
5. The dog or puppy goes into a squatting posture.
• If the puppy can't wait, gently, calmly, but quickly pick it up and go to the relief spot even if it has an accident. At the relief spot, wait until the pup defecates or urinates there and then praise it enthusiastically.
• Thoroughly clean any soiled spots and make use of scent removers as canines are motivated to use a spot where the smell of previous urine or feces remains.
• *Never* speak harshly or punish the puppy at the relief spot for any reason. This is a place where the puppy needs lots of little victories and rewards of praise from you. Don't confuse the youngster with correction at this special site.
• *Never* rub a puppy's nose in its messes. This does nothing positive for the puppy's learning and only gets it dirty.
• *Never* strike a puppy with

Great aids to housebreaking your pup are automatic outside visits after eating or drinking, late at night, and first thing each morning.

your hand, a rolled-up newspaper, or anything else! This especially applies to a natural activity like defecating or urinating. This will only make the pup fear you and will actually slow down learning.

• Screaming at a puppy in the act of making a mess in the house is futile. You might gain some time to get the youngster outside by clapping your hands and saying a firm "No," which may break its concentration on making a mess. Rush the pup outside and praise it when it goes where it should.

• Feed a high-quality puppy food that provides excellent digestibility. The stools with this kind of food will generally be smaller and firmer, an added benefit if an accident does happen, and easier for the pup to "hold."

• Avoid snacks and table scraps. This will not only unbalance the pup's diet, but will hinder your effort to time when trips outside should occur.

• Don't leave food in the Amstaff or APBT pup's food bowl all day long. This will also throw off your relief trip schedule and pups generally do better on several small meals each day.

Another sign of needing to go outside is squatting behavior, especially near the door. Again, hurry the puppy to the right place for it to void its waste.

• Don't put food or edible toys like dog biscuits in the crate. Let the crate be a place of rest and/or confinement and have somewhere else for food.

• Don't leave your American pit bull terrier or Amstaff puppy overly long in its crate as this will be painful for the youngster that may try to keep from voiding waste in order to keep the den area clean.

• Be consistent with your housebreaking efforts and see that others in your household are also. Consistent training will teach most American Staffordshires or APBTs what housebreaking is all about.

• If you have a fenced backyard, never just turn a puppy out alone to relieve itself. Your praise is the reward for going at the right place and the right time.

• Playtime should not begin outside until the pup has used the relief area. Going outside must signify waste relief and not play to the youngster.

- Because puppies naturally will not want to urinate or defecate near their food, water, and sleeping areas, these should be as far away from the waste area as possible.
- Because it is less effective, whenever possible reward with praise the immediate use of the waste area (as you would if the pup were at the relief spot outside).
- Paper training and outside visits early in the morning and late at night can be combined. Always be lavish with praise if the puppy defecates or urinates outside.
- A further way to combine the lesser effective paper method with the more effective use of an outside area is to make the waste area in the confinement room smaller and smaller as the pup matures. Gradually a pup or young dog can be transferred completely outside. This will require a complete deodorizing of the room and a shift to the crate training/outside trip method.

Crate Training

Crate training works because your Amstaff or APBT puppy almost instinctively will not want to mess up its den or sleeping area. The puppy will normally learn this behavior from its mother who would chastise an older puppy who made a mess in the litter's sleeping quarters. In the wild, canines don't want to let the smell of feces and urine be a draw for predators, so denning areas are not normally fouled with urine and feces. Crate training takes advantage of two very strong innate behaviors: 1. denning behavior and 2. the desire to keep a den area clean. By encouraging these behaviors, you can make crate training not only convenient and useful for you but natural and comfortable for your pet. Some things to remember about crate training are:
- Keep a positive attitude about crates. Knowledgeable dog owners know that

the crate is a place of refuge for a puppy or a dog, not a cruel prison.
- When you purchase a cage/crate/carrier for your Amstaff or American pit pull terrier, bear in mind that the small puppy of today will be the sturdy, medium-sized dog of the near future. Buy a crate for the adult dog! Use temporary partitions, usually available where you bought the crate or easily made, to keep the crate the right size for a growing puppy. If the crate is too large, the puppy may develop a waste elimination area in the corner away from where it sleeps. Keep the crate just big enough for the growing youngster.
- Place the crate in an out-of-the-way, but not an isolated, place in your home. This location must be away from highly changeable temperature fluctuations, drafts, and direct sunshine.
- Put the puppy in its den when it needs to rest and for a few hours when you will not be around to supervise it. Always take the puppy out of the crate and outside as soon as you return home.
- Taking the puppy out of the crate should not become a reward. Don't praise the youngster (except at the relief spot outside) for 10 or 15 minutes after you let it out of the crate.
- Make the crate comfortable for the pup by placing a sleeping mat in the crate. These mats are made to fit every size of cage, crate, or carrier and come in many washable colors and designs.
- Do not put food or water in the crate. This will only promote a messy sleeping area, and food and water are best kept elsewhere.
- If the youngster whines, barks, or cries in the crate, use a calm, authoritative voice to quiet the puppy (see Helping Your APBT/Amstaff Pup Settle In, page 54).
- Be certain that all members of your household understand what the

crate does and what crate training is all about.

• While training your pup, return it to the crate for a half-hour "break" before letting it out for a play session. This will imprint on the puppy that training is serious and not just part of playtime.

Basic Training

Your American pit bull terrier or American Staffordshire terrier will need early and consistent training. By remembering that some puppies mature faster than others, you will be able to find a good time to begin a more serious approach to teaching your pup the basic things it must learn.

Because some strains or families within the American Staffordshire terriers and American pit bull terriers have different levels of maturation and trainability, you will want to involve your breeder/mentor in helping you decide when to begin with your puppy. Because these breeds often need very early work to get them off to a good start, you will need this friend's opinion on how your particular pup is progressing.

It is also true that potential training concerns may surface in different Amstaff or APBT lines. Some strains are known to be more animal aggressive than others. Listen to the advice of the breed experts that you have come to know about how best to initiate training with your puppy.

There are five basic commands that you will want your American pit bull terrier or Amstaff to learn. These commands will give you a good level of control over your young puppy, which is a crucial element to successful ownership of a dog of one of these breeds. These commands are: "Sit," "Stay," "Heel," "Down," and "Come." Each of these commands involves a little bit different level of training. Each will be useful in everyday pet ownership.

The Essentials of Training Your Puppy

Establish a regular training schedule each day: Training sessions don't have to be long. Between 10 and 15 minutes for each session is long enough.

Keep the sessions geared toward training: Avoid places and times when there are distractions that could draw away the full attention of your puppy. Although these times should be enjoyable, they are not times for play.

Fill the "alpha" role: The firm, businesslike sound of your voice will let the puppy know training time is different from playtime and that you are in charge. Be stern and consistent, but remember to never attempt training when you are angry or upset over something.

Set clear and attainable training goals: Before each training session, set definite, but reasonable, things you want to accomplish in this session. Don't expect too much too soon. Make training a matter of small, incremental steps that will ultimately move you and your Amstaff/APBT puppy toward a specific direction. (Training hint: Go over with your family what each training session is going to try to teach your puppy. Make sure they understand that they can confuse and set back the progress of a youngster by doing things that undo the training.)

Conduct each session as a single-focus class: You know that your APBT or American Staffordshire terrier may not respond well to a lot of meaningless repetition of commands. You also know that each session must have a beginning point and an ending point. Try to end each session in a positive way.

Stick to your planned goals for that session: When you train your puppy, you can go back over previous lessons, but if the goal for today is heeling, focus on heeling. Correct your pup each time it does not heel correctly and praise it each time it does it right. If your APBT or Amstaff pup begins to chafe with the repetitions, cut the session short.

Reward the right way: Although some animal trainers use small bits of food as a reward during training, most dog trainers recognize that praise is what the dog wants most. When a youngster correctly does what it was commanded to do, give it an enthusiastic pat and warm word of praise. Doing the right thing once does not mean that you and your puppy can begin playtime.

Separate training time from fun time: You want to keep your pup's attention on what it must learn. Put a little distance in the pup's mind between the training session and any subsequent play. Praise a trainee for doing the right thing but wait until later to show lavish affection as you play with your beloved pet.

Follow the mother dog's example of correcting immediately: Like the mother dog, you should make corrections right then, right on the spot. Waiting to correct a puppy later is useless because the youngster may not even remember the correction involved.

Consistency—the key to good training: You may only be an amateur training your first dog, but if you are consistent, doing the training the same way each time, you will get better results than an experienced professional who is inconsistent. The young dog will need to know that the stern alpha voice you use during training means that this is serious. If you use a different tone or different words in the basic commands, the puppy may never know what you are implying.

Patience is the greatest virtue in training: As important as consistency is, without patience you are lost. Regardless of how good an American pit bull terrier or Amstaff puppy you think you have, it is still just a puppy. It may want to learn from you to gain your praise, but if you push it faster than it can go you could ruin a fine young animal. Always be patient, both with your pup and with yourself as a trainer.

Avoid immediate training sessions after long periods of crate confinement: Puppies will usually have a lot of pent-up energy at this time and will find it hard to concentrate on their lessons.

The Right Training Equipment

Training equipment for your Amstaff/APBT will consist of the following items:

A training collar: Commonly misnamed a "choke" collar, the training collar is both humane and effective when used correctly and appropriately. This collar is for use *only* during training sessions. When correcting pressure is applied with a slight snap, the dog's head will come up and its attention will be brought back to the training. Combined with a stern "No," this training collar not only controls and corrects, it lets the pup know that it did something wrong. This collar should be large enough to go over the widest part of your puppy's head with no more than an inch leeway. This collar is, as stated, *not* for regular wear. It is important that the puppy associates the training collar with the serious business of learning. This chain collar also could become snagged on something and cause the youngster to be injured.

A training leash (or lead): Along with the training collar, you will need to purchase a 1-inch (2.5 cm) wide lead (commonly called a leash) that will not be used on your regular walks with your Amstaff or APBT pup. This, like the training collar, is just for training and should be made of leather, nylon, or woven web material. It should be 6 feet

The training collar is used only for training and should not be left on the puppy at other times.

Firmness: Give one-word commands in a clear voice to your dog always using the dog's name before each command to get its attention: "Gunnar, sit." Be firm and businesslike. Don't talk babytalk or use pet nicknames. Playtime is later. This is training time.

Consistency: As in so many other areas of APBT/Amstaff ownership, consistency here is very important. Use the same tone of voice each and every time so that your tone as well as your voice will reinforce the seriousness of this training time.

Be specific—don't issue a string of several commands at one time: "Gunnar, come here and sit down." This will only confuse the dog. Each command should be a single, specific word pronounced the same way and in the same tone each time.

Use the mother model: Remember that the puppy's first training came from a real expert, its mother. Follow her example to:
1. Correct misbehavior immediately.
2. Be consistent.
3. Never lose your temper.
4. Reward with enthusiastic praise.
5. Always be patient.

(1.8 m) long, be of very sturdy construction, and have a comfortable and strong hand loop on one end. On the other end should be a brass or stainless steel swivel snap that can be attached to the ring on the training collar.

Let your puppy become thoroughly familiar with both the collar and the lead before you actually begin using them. These two items are important tools of the dog trainer's trade and should be of good quality. It is important that the Amstaff or American pit bull terrier puppy not fear or dislike these tools, but that they should signify that training time is here.

The Five Key Commands

Before You Begin Training

Just like a drill sergeant about to train some new soldiers, you need to have a "command voice" to best get your orders across. Before you begin training, you will need to develop such a voice to differentiate from you as a trainer and you as the pup's pal. Practice the following verbal skills:

The Sit

Because your puppy will already know how to sit, your main role is to teach it when to sit and where to sit. The "sit" is a good first lesson for your puppy to learn because so many other basic and even some of the advanced obedience commands begin or end in this natural position.

The training collar should be around the pup's neck and correctly attached to the leash or lead. Start the "sit" with the youngster on your left, next to your left leg. Take up all but about 12 inches (30 cm) of the excess lead. Hold the lead in your right hand. In a smooth, continuous, gentle, but firm upward move, lift the puppy's head so

In one continuous, gentle motion, pull the puppy's head up as you push its hindquarters down, giving the firm verbal command "Sit" as you do so.

that it is facing a little above horizontal. As you do so, press downward on the pup's hindquarters gently. The lift of its head combined with the pushing down on its hindquarters will force the young dog to sit down as you give the command, "Gunnar, sit."

Be careful not to push down on the pup's rear end hard enough to injure or frighten the youngster. You only want to make it sit, not hurt it. After the puppy does sit, give it lots of praise. Just like with doing its business at the relief spot, you want the puppy to associate the praise with the action. This is the basis of dog training.

Try the "sit" several times, remembering the three important parts: 1. slight upward pressure on the lead and collar to lift up the pup's head; 2. gentle downward pressure on the pup's hindquarters; and 3. the "sit" command given at exactly the same time you do the other two. Don't overdo the first few sessions and don't

keep a puppy sitting too long or tire it or bore it by a great many repetitions. Keep the sessions interesting and enjoyable for the puppy.

Your bright American Staffordshire or American pit bull terrier puppy will probably catch on to the "sit" very quickly. When the pup does, it will want to gain your approval and your praise and will soon be sitting on its own, even without the lead and training collar!

The Stay

After your APBT/Amstaff has mastered the "sit," it is ready for the next command, the "stay." This command actually begins with your pup in the "sit" and really can't be learned until the first lesson is firmly a part of what your young dog knows.

The "stay" begins with the puppy sitting next to your left leg. The lead is again in your right hand and is used to hold the head of the youngster up. Using your firm, alpha voice, give the command "Gunnar, stay" as you step straight forward away from the sitting puppy, leading with your right foot. At the same time, bring the palm of your left hand down in front of the young dog's face in a reverse of the well-known police hand signal for "stop."

The "stay" will require four coordinated parts done at precisely the same time: 1. your gentle lifting pressure on the lead to keep the pup's head up; 2. your step forward, beginning with your right foot; 3. your left hand being placed, palm downward, in front of the dog's face; and 4. your clear, firm vocal command, "Stay."

The "stay" is a conflicting command for a youngster. It loves you and wants to be with you, but it wants to please you by doing what you want. The "stay" forces the pup to choose pleasing you over staying with you.

Some American Staffordshire terrier or American pit bull terrier puppies will easily learn the "stay," but others will have some trouble with it. If your pup doesn't stay at first, don't overdo this command the first few "stay" training sessions. You can try it several times, if the puppy has trouble, go back to a few "sits" and let the puppy end each session with some successes and the praise reward these successes should always bring.

Patience is needed in teaching a very young dog this conflicting command. Take your time. Remember this is just a young puppy you are working with. Be consistent in how you give the command, pull up on the lead, step away, and put your palm in front of the pup's face. Your efforts will pay off and your puppy will "stay."

The length of the "stay" a puppy executes may not be very long at first, but gradually the puppy will learn to stay where you want it to and you can move further and further away. Remember to praise the puppy for any length of "stay."

Once the pup can handle this fairly tough command, you can insert a cheerfully given release word, "Okay," which will let the puppy know that it can do what it really wants and come to you and be rewarded.

The Heel

Being able to walk with your pet at the correct place by your left leg will be a useful thing for a young puppy to know. The "heel" takes on added importance with the American pit bull terrier and the Amstaff because these dogs are often real pullers. Teaching a very young APBT or American Staffordshire not to attempt to drag you along behind it is a crucially important skill. You will be able to control the pulling and tugging of a little pup, but a 60-pound (27.2 kg) dog can probably tow all children and most adults. The time to teach the "heel" is while you still have the upper hand and are stronger than your terrier.

Giving the clear, firm command "Stay," step away from the sitting puppy, moving your right foot first. At the same time, bring the palm of your left hand down in front of the pup's face.

Like the "stay," the "heel" begins in the "sit" position. Both the "sit" and the "stay" must be mastered by your pup before you should attempt to teach heeling.

Hold the lead, still attached to the training collar, in your right hand. The puppy should be sitting alongside your left foot. As you give the clear, alpha-voiced command, "Gunnar, heel," step off, leading with your left foot this time. If the puppy doesn't move forward when you do, pop the leftover loop of the lead loudly against the side of your left leg and keep on walking. The lack of your palm in its face, plus your movement with the left foot rather than the right, combined with the gentle forward pull of the lead on its collar should cause the pup to move along with you.

When the puppy starts walking with you, praise it, but keep on moving. Keep praising the youngster as long as it stays with you, right by your left side. If the puppy has problems with this command, don't drag it all over the yard attempting to get it moving. Start the "heel" lesson again by going

Holding the training leash in your right hand and leading off with your left foot, step forward while calling the dog by name and firmly saying "Heel."

back to the sitting and staying positions and following the steps of the command: 1. holding the lead in your right hand, with the pup at a sit, step out with your *left* foot; 2. using a firm voice, give the "heel" command; 3. gently applying forward pressure on the lead. If the pup does not move, snap the lead sharply against your leg to get its attention and keep moving; and 4. praising on the move and continuing the praise only as long as the pup moves with you.

When you stop, give the "sit" command. The puppy will want to walk along with you, and as the "heel" makes this possible, it should be fairly easy for your Amstaff/APBT to learn. Teach the "heel" the right way each time, correcting the puppy immediately if it tries to lag behind you, or branch off in another direction, or run on ahead of you. You have to be the one who will choose where you walk and how fast you will go. As with other lessons, make this enjoyable, but be consistent and patient.

The Down

The "down" command has its beginnings with the "sit" and the "stay." It has some aspects of the "stay" in that you want the pup to remain in this one spot. It is different than the "stay" in that you use downward pressure on the lead this time, instead of upward pressure. You want the pup's head and torso to go down to the ground or floor and for it to lie on its stomach.

Using your right hand, pull down on the lead while making a strong, repeated downward motion (not unlike slowly bouncing a basketball) in front of the dog's face. At the same time you do these two things, you give the clear, firm command using the dog's name as in "Gunnar, down."

When the puppy has reached the belly-on-the-ground position, heap on the praise. The "down" is made easier because it is a natural position that the pup already knows. Your role is to teach the pup to do the "down" when you command it to do so. The constant, but gentle downward pull of the lead in your hand will force the young dog to comply with your wishes.

The "down" is another command that must be taught to the APBT/Amstaff while you still have the leverage and greater power to teach it. It is possible that you could have quite a time trying to teach the "down" to an adult American Staffordshire or American pit bull terrier that didn't want to do it. Start young to make this command as automatic as possible.

Your goal in this command is to be able to get your puppy and later your adult dog to go down on its stomach upon hearing you give the verbal command and to stay there until you have given the "Okay" release word. This command can only be taught by a consistent and patient trainer.

When the puppy starts obeying this command, don't intentionally or accidentally abuse the "down" by leaving a youngster in the position longer than a few minutes. Gradually you can lengthen the "down" periods. Keep the early sessions short and fun for the dog. Later the "down" should be like the "stay" with the dog remaining in position (no swiveling around or rolling over on its back) until the release word is given. If the puppy doesn't stay down or moves around, correct it. When it does do a good "down," for however long, provide a reward of praise.

The Come

All dogs know how to come to their master or mistress, don't they? This may be true when the dog itself wants to come to you, but the "come" is very important in that it stresses that the young APBT/Amstaff is to come to you, each and every time you give the command.

Along with patience and consistency, the "come" will require enthusiasm from you. You should always call the dog by name, "Gunnar, come!" When beginning your teaching of this command, let cheerfulness blend with your firmness of voice. Make this command to a very young puppy an invitation to come to the person it loves. Spread your arms out wide and call the puppy to you using the appropriate command. When the youngster does what it really wants to do, that is come to be with you, give it a lot of praise.

The "come" can be misused and a puppy or dog actually taught to ignore the command. *Never* call your APBT/Amstaff to you to punish it or reprimand it! Never allow anyone in your household to do this. The puppy must associate the command to "come" with a happy outcome when it obeys, not with the possibility that it will be punished or scolded for something. As you should never scold or reprimand a puppy or dog at the special waste relief site, you should never use the "come" to get the animal

The "Down" command involves gently pulling the pup's head and chest downward while firmly saying "Down" and moving your hand in a repeated downward motion.

within reach so you can do something it will not like. If you need to punish or reprimand, *you go to the dog*, don't try to make it come to you.

One way to teach the "come" to a young and possibly inattentive puppy is by using the regular lead, or even a longer training lead of 20 feet (6.1 m) or more attached to the training collar. Exert gentle pressure in bringing the pup toward you combined with the happy, enthusiastic "come" command with the lavish praise reward for the pup when it obeys.

Never underestimate the vital importance of the "come" command and your American pit bull terrier or Amstaff's immediate obedience to it. This one command, if instantly obeyed, can keep a young or headstrong dog from trouble or even death. An Amstaff or an APBT that will not come immediately on command should never be allowed off a leash or out of a fenced backyard or kennel.

"Come" is a command that is best taught with the use of a longer leash. Always praise the puppy when it comes on call. Never call a dog to you for punishment, as this will confuse your pet.

Don't use the "come" command too much as the puppy could become bored or jaded at numerous repetitions of it. One good way to use it is to surprise the puppy when it is doing something else, playing or running in the backyard. Give the "come" command when the youngster isn't expecting it and then heap on the praise for quick obedience.

Obedience Classes to Help You *and* Your Dog

Although your training efforts will normally be sufficient, you should avail yourself of any dog training classes that are in your area. Not only will you and your pup learn more quickly, you will do so with experienced trainers who have dealt with any problems that may arise for you and your pet. These training classes are usually held at night in some easily accessible place and have much to offer you and your American Staffordshire or American pit bull terrier.

Your puppy will gain socialization skills by being around other humans who like and understand young dogs. It will be given exposure to other dogs that are there for the same training. This will give you a chance to observe, under tightly controlled conditions, the level of animal aggressive tendencies that your young APBT/Amstaff may have. This is an extremely valuable piece of information for you to have!

One lifelong breeder of dual-registered American pit bull terriers and American Staffordshire terriers made this observation pertaining to obedience classes: "I highly recommend them to even the most experienced dog owners who are getting an Amstaff (or APBT) for the first time and I absolutely will not sell a puppy to a first-time dog owner unless they agree to faithfully attend classes."

Your APBT/Amstaff Terrier and Medical Care

Developing a Wellness Plan for Your Dog

Good health for your American pit bull terrier or American Staffordshire terrier will not just happen. You need to be proactive to keep your dog healthy and to shield it from injury. Your pet will give you devotion, affection, and fun-filled hours, but it will have to depend solely on you to keep it healthy and safe.

Your Amstaff/APBT will deserve a carefully considered plan to keep it in good shape and let it live out its natural life span. Don't leave the health of this trusting, canine member of your family to chance. Concentrate on discovering those things that can harm your pet and then eliminate or deal with them. You may not be able to do this without the help of some other knowledgeable people.

A Health Care Team

The American pit bull terrier or Amstaff puppy that you have invited into your home will greatly benefit from a group of concerned humans who have its best health interests at heart. On this team could be:
• You, and the members of your family, who will be the first line of defense for your puppy in so many areas. You will choose a pet from a strain or family that is as free as possible from genetically transmitted diseases and uncertain temperament. You will

puppy-proof your home to prevent accidents to a curious and ignorant puppy. You will provide adequate housing, fencing, training, and other controls to keep your pet from hurting itself or others. You will obtain top-quality veterinary care, food, and knowledgeable advice to help your pup grow into a healthy, well-adjusted adult. You will share your lives with this dog and love it and let it love you.
• An experienced Amstaff/APBT breeder will serve as a friend/mentor and help you learn to become a responsible, aware dog owner. This knowledgeable person will perform the valuable function of seeing your pet often enough to recognize traits and other specific things about it, but rarely enough to be objective about certain aspects of the dog's health, training, or care. This APBT/Amstaff mentor will help you know the best paths to take in helping your pet reach its potential—in the show ring, in obedience trials, as potential breeding stock, or as a first-class family pet.
• Your veterinarian will be the fulcrum on which the health of your American Staffordshire terrier or American pit bull terrier may balance. Find a veterinarian who knows and likes these dogs and has some experience with them. (This shouldn't be hard, as veterinarians are often some of the staunchest supporters of the APBT/Amstaff). Depend on this

professional's expertise in immunization, health problem prevention, and treatment. Follow the suggestions, prescription instructions, and treatment plans worked out by your veterinarian.

Prevention of Accidents

Much of the preventive focus depends on common sense, on anticipating problems, and moving to head them off. Puppy-proofing is one form of accident prevention. Keeping your APBT/Amstaff under the control of sturdy fencing, strong leashes and collars, and good training is another facet of stopping accidents before they happen. Spaying and neutering pet-quality Amstaffs and American pit bull terriers can be accident prevention, in several senses of the term.

Keeping your terrier out of potentially dangerous spots (like a parked car on a warm day or running off-leash in a city park) is definitely accident prevention. Recognizing that animal aggression is part of the genetic makeup of some Amstaffs or APBTs and dealing with this before problems occur is also in this category. Recognizing that dogs of these two breeds tend to drown

Be certain that you and your veterinarian keep your puppy up-to-date with its immunizations. This could save the youngster's life!

more often than do many other breeds can lead an owner to prevent this senseless type of fatality. Protecting your Amstaff/APBT puppy or adult from becoming poisoned from common household chemicals is good accident prevention.

Prevention of Illnesses

Your American pit bull terrier or American Staffordshire terrier is an extremely short-coated breed and may suffer from cold weather more acutely than some other breeds. Protect your pet from cold temperatures by letting it live indoors with you or, if it must stay in an outside kennel, by providing a thoroughly insulated and draft-proof doghouse.

You and your veterinarian can help eliminate much in the way of parasites and, in so doing, eliminate some of the health problems that can stem from flea, tick, and worm infestation. You can do your part at home to keep your pet away from unhygienic conditions and away from stray animals that may harbor communicable illnesses.

Immunizations

Getting your Amstaff or APBT immunized against the wide spectrum of illnesses that attack canines is a key part of your wellness plan for your pet. In some cases, these shots are not options but are mandated by law.

Your American Staffordshire terrier or APBT may have had its first immunizations when it was about six weeks old. These shots may have been administered while the puppy was still under the breeder's care and you should have a clearly annotated record of just what shots your new pet had at that time. The first round of immunizations were vaccinations for distemper and measles and possibly for parvovirus, canine hepatitis, leptospirosis, parainfluenza, coronavirus and also bordetella.

Even if your youngster was immunized for all these illnesses, it will still need follow-up shots at eight to ten weeks, again at 12 weeks, and normally ending the puppy immunizations, another group of shots at 16 to 18 weeks.

Note: A number of experienced American Staffordshire and American pit bull terrier breeders assert that pups of these breeds may need even additional immunization protection due to what they believe is a breed characteristic that makes young Amstaffs and APBTs harder to immunize. This is an area of concern that can best be discussed with your veterinarian and your knowledgeable breeder-mentor.

When you take your new puppy to the veterinarian for the first time, take along its medical record that the breeder should have supplied. Your dog's doctor will need to know what immunizations and other treatments this puppy may have received. Take care of these early documents as they form the nucleus of what should be your pet's lifelong health records.

When your veterinarian sets up an immunization schedule for your young APBT or American Staffordshire, follow it with the greatest of care. The best puppy from the best breeder, out of the best strain of American pit bull terriers or Amstaffs, can die in an amazingly short time if you have not been diligent in getting immunizations done at the recommended times.

Distemper

One of the oldest enemies of the canine, wild and domestic, is distemper. At one time, this widespread and extremely infectious viral killer was the greatest known threat to puppies and young dogs. Entire kennels were wiped out by distemper.

There is today an immunization program that has greatly decreased the incidence of distemper. Distemper, although more controlled now than decades ago, is still deadly when it has not been immunized against. Distemper is still very much in evidence among wild canines and in places where vaccination for it is inadequate or nonexistent.

A dog not completely immunized against distemper may show clinical signs as early as a week after being near an animal with the disease. At first, distemper looks like a cold with a runny nose accompanied by a slight fever. Dogs will often stop eating and exhibit fatigue, listlessness, and diarrhea.

Rabies

Rabies is one of those diseases that brings about nightmares of loving pets being transformed into ravening, foam-at-the-mouth, canine demons bent on biting any and everything around them. Rabies is made all the more frightening because it can be transmitted to humans and to most other warm-blooded mammals by the saliva of an infected animal, which is usually passed by a bite. In 1885, the French scientist Louis Pasteur developed a vaccine for this great dread. Until Pasteur, rabies meant certain death in the most hideous manner imaginable!

One of the classic indicators of rabies was supposed to be the other name by which this dread killer is known—hydrophobia or "fear of water." Paralysis of the laryngeal muscles that control swallowing will bring on excessive salivation or "foaming at the mouth." The dog does not fear water as much as it is unable to drink and swallow.

Rabies in companion animals is fairly uncommon now due to an aggressive immunization plan. It still occurs in populations of wild animals, skunks, raccoons, foxes, and stray or feral dogs and cats. England has been able to largely eliminate any incidence of rabies because of its natural

This Welsh corgi seems to be showing the youngster around.

oceanic boundaries and because of a vigorous quarantine that kept out many potential carriers.

There are two stages or phases of rabies. The first, often called the furious phase is so named because the inflicted animal may attack anything with which it comes in contact. Some animals die while still in the furious mode, but others live to go into the second phase. This is often called the dumb phase, which ultimately ends in paralysis, unconsciousness, and finally death.

Failure to keep a dog immunized against such an infectious and horrible killer is negligent and unlawful. Protect your puppy, your family, and yourself by making certain that your puppy gets immunized at three to six months of age. Also be sure that your pet gets its second shot at about one year of age with annual to triennial shots for the rest of the dog's life!

Leptospirosis

Leptospirosis is a bacterial disease that primarily does damage to the infected dog's kidneys. In advanced cases, it can severely injure both the liver and the kidneys, causing jaundice, sores in the dog's mouth, a loss in weight, and a general weakening of the dog's hindquarters.

Leptospirosis is commonly spread by drinking water contaminated by an animal with the disease. Clinical signs of this illness are loss of appetite, fever, diarrhea, abdominal pain, and vomiting. Immunization followed by an annual booster shot will protect your pet from leptospirosis.

Hepatitis

Infectious canine hepatitis is not the same illness that humans can contract. The canine version can affect any member of the Canis family and can range in severity from a deadly viral infection that can kill a dog within one day's time after it is diagnosed, to a fairly mild disease.

This infectious disease can be spread by coming in contact with the urine or feces of a dog inflicted with infectious canine hepatitis. Clinical signs of the illness are listlessness, abdominal pain, tonsillitis, increased light sensitivity, fever, and bloody stools and/or vomitus.

Infectious canine hepatitis can be prevented by a good immunization program followed up by annual boosters.

Parvovirus

Young puppies especially fall victim to parvovirus, but this viral disease can take the life of an unimmunized dog at any age! Parvovirus primarily attacks the immune system, gastrointestinal tract, and heart, along with the bone marrow. Young animals with this disease can suffer severe dehydration due to profuse bloody and watery diarrhea and vomiting. From onset of the disease, parvovirus can kill an affected dog or puppy within 48 hours.

Immediate medical care can save some parvovirus-stricken dogs and puppies from death, but an effective immunization program can spare most from ever contracting the disease. Annual boosters should follow a puppy vaccination for parvovirus.

Parainfluenza

This highly contagious virus can spread rapidly through a litter of puppies or through a home with several dogs. Parainfluenza is thought to be spread by contact with infected animals, as well as through the air. This disease causes tracheobronchitis, which causes a dry, hacking cough followed by repeated attempts to cough up mucus.

Parainfluenza alone is not usually very serious. If tracheobronchitis is left untreated, it can sufficiently weaken a victim and leave it vulnerable to other infections. The best course of action with parainfluenza is immunization in the puppy series of shots followed by annual reinforcement by booster.

A dog or puppy with parainfluenza is usually treated by a veterinarian in isolated conditions to prevent the spread of this disease.

Coronavirus

Both puppies and adult dogs of all ages can become victims of coronavirus. This contagious disease, which is characterized by severe diarrhea with loose, foul-smelling watery stools tinged with blood, can rapidly debilitate a dog or puppy. In a condition weakened by coronavirus, an afflicted animal can contract parvovirus or other infections. An Amstaff or American pit bull terrier with coronavirus can be successfully treated, but prevention through immunization is again the best course.

Bordetella

The bacterial infection bordetella often comes along with a bout of tracheobronchitis. When a bordetella infection is present, it can complicate the treatment for tracheobronchitis. An immunization can usually prevent or lessen the severity of both bordetella and the parainfluenza infections that cause tracheobronchitis.

Borelliosis (Lyme Disease)

Borelliosis, or Lyme disease, affects many mammals including humans. It is a serious, potentially fatal illness that is believed to be spread primarily by the tiny deer tick to dogs or to dog owners.

Originally identified in and named for Lyme, Connecticut, this disease, which carries the medical name of borelliosis, has now spread to many parts of the United States. At one time, only hunters and hunting dogs were considered prime candidates to be infected, but you or your dog could contract this ailment in a city park or even in a suburban backyard.

Clinical signs of Lyme disease include swelling and tenderness around joints, and a loss of appetite. If you or your APBT/Amstaff have been bitten by any tick, you would be wise to seek a professional medical and veterinary opinion as soon as possible!

Other Possible Health Problems

Anal Sac Impaction

On either side of a dog's anus lie the anal glands. Normal defecation usually empties these glands but sometimes they become clogged or impacted. When impaction occurs, these glands must be emptied of their strong-smelling secretions by hand.

One sure sign of anal gland impaction is the scooting motion seen in an affected dog as it drags its rear end along the floor. Your veterinarian can handle this concern, or you can easily learn to do it yourself.

Diarrhea

Some diarrhea is common in dogs and puppies. It may be caused by stress, food changes, or internal parasites. Diarrhea can also signal the onset of some serious illness. Any diarrhea that continues for more than 12 to 24 hours should alert you to the need of a trip with your pet to the veterinarian.

Vomiting

Like diarrhea, some vomiting is to be expected. Excitement in pups after eating may bring it on. A change in diet or added stress may cause vomiting.

Also like diarrhea, vomiting can be a signal that something more serious may be happening within your dog or puppy. Vomiting and diarrhea can lead to dehydration, which can put a young pup's life in peril rather quickly. Any vomiting that continues over an extended period (more than 12 hours) should trigger an automatic visit to the veterinary clinic.

Bloat (Gastric Torsion)

Bloat, or gastric torsion, is a very serious health concern for all deep-chested breeds of dogs, which includes the American Staffordshire terrier and the American pit bull terrier.

Bloat can painfully kill an otherwise healthy dog in just a few hours. It involves a swelling and torsion (or twisting) of the dog's stomach from water or gas or both.

Bloat is still somewhat of a mystery ailment. There are a lot of suggested causes that may work independently of each other or that may combine to cause bloating. Some of these are:
• A large meal, particularly of dry dog food, followed by a large intake of water, followed by strenuous exercise.
• A genetic predisposition in some breeds and even within some strains or families within a breed.
• Stress from any of several sources.
• The age of the dog. Dogs over 24 months old seem to be more likely to bloat than do younger animals.
• The gender of a dog. Males seem to be more affected by bloat than do females.

From whatever cause, bloat is a real killer of deep-chested dogs. Although the American pit bull terrier and the Amstaff are apparently not quite as susceptible as bloodhounds, Great Danes, and some others, enough APBTs and Amstaffs die from bloat to make it something you will want to know about. Some clinical signs of bloat are:
• Obvious abdominal pain and noticeable abdominal swelling.
• Excessive salivation and rapid breathing.
• Pale and cool-to-the-touch skin in the mouth.
• A dazed and "shocky" look.
• Multiple attempts to vomit, especially when nothing comes up.

A dog with bloat needs immediate care if it is to stand a chance of survival. First, alert your veterinarian; then safely transport your dog to the clinic.

Canine Hip Dysplasia

One of the most discussed and cussed canine health issues for modern dog owners is CHD, or canine hip dysplasia. CHD does not have the life-threatening immediacy of many of the common canine diseases or of gastric tortion (bloat), but it can be quite debilitating and painful for a dog that has a severe form of this condition.

By description, CHD is a medical condition in which the hip joint is slack or loose. This slackness or looseness is combined with a deformity of the socket of the hip and the femoral head joining the thighbone. This malformation of the development of the hip's bone and connective tissues leaves an instable hip joint. Instead of a strong fit like a cup for the end of the thighbone, the CHD-affected hip is often quite shallow. This condition can cause an unsteady, wobbling gait that can be very painful.

Much has been written about the possibility of CHD being an inherited disorder. This may be only partially accurate, for not every puppy born of a dysplastic sire and/or dam will have the condition. It is conversely also true that even "normal" or non-CHD parents can produce some dysplastic offspring.

CHD cannot be determined with any degree of certainty until a dog is around two years old. The Orthopedic Foundation for Animals (OFA) has developed a widely used X-ray process that is used to determine if CHD is present in a dog and the degree to which it is present. Some veterinarians may also be able to pre-screen for CHD by using the Penn hip testing method on younger dogs.

American Staffordshire terriers are fairly high on the list of breeds that have a relatively high incidence of hip dysplasia. There is some disagreement among American pit bull terrier and American Staffordshire terrier breeders about just how valid the CHD testing is for their dogs. One breeder asserted that many APBTs and Amstaffs that are judged to have CHD by the OFA testing never seem to develop CHD. A prominent Amstaff breeder (of double-registered dogs) produced an OFA test for a particular American Staffordshire that was significantly worse than an OFA test on the same dog submitted for testing as an American pit bull terrier!

Regardless of whether some breeders are more prone to believe their dogs are not afflicted with CHD quite to the degree that testing may seem to indicate, CHD should be a matter of concern. The better the CHD test scores on your pup's parents, the better your chances seem to be of getting a youngster that won't be crippled by this painful condition. CHD is just another reason for taking your time when you set out to find the right American pit bull terrier or American Staffordshire terrier puppy.

Allergies, Skin, and Coat Problems

Some dogs in every breed seem to become the victim of every allergy and skin or coat problem that comes along. The presence of inherited conditions is something that you will want to avoid in the puppy of your choice. One reason for seeing the parents of your puppy is to personally assess their appearance. Other than the wear and tear that you should expect on the coat of a brood bitch that has just gone through pregnancy and puppy raising, the parents should look good.

There are some colors within the American pit bull terrier and American Staffordshire terrier breeds that may tend to have more skin problems than others. It is thought that the dilute colors—blue, chocolate (or liver), and cream—may be more susceptible to skin worries than others. This is not always the case, but dilute colors do, in all breeds where they occur, tend to prove out this hypothesis.

What you feed your pet may contribute to the presence of skin conditions.

Some ingredients are said to produce rashes or "hot spots" in some dogs and even in some breeds.

Washing your APBT or Amstaff too often will promote a dry coat and flaky skin. It is also true that poor housing and poorly maintained hygiene can contribute to skin problems. Stress and allergies to common household chemicals can cause skin and coat problems.

By and large most American pit bull terriers and most American Staffordshire terriers are not plagued with the high percentages of allergic reactions and poor skin and coats with which some other breeds must contend. Choosing the right breeder and the right stock from which to choose your puppy will usually help you avoid most inherited skin concerns.

Some APBTs and Amstaffs will have severe reactions to insect bites. Bee stings, and ant bites can cause excessive swelling and possible death for some dogs. Watch for these reactions and rush your pet to the veterinarian.

Inherited Conditions

Because much of their fairly recent history involved the necessity for superb physical conditioning, both the American Staffordshire terrier and the American pit bull terrier don't have much of a legacy of poor inheritance. Because their ancestry had to survive under the toughest of circumstances, until the recent flush of popularity, these breeds didn't have poor-quality specimens serving as breeding stock.

Some closely bred (line or inbred) strains or families may be more prone to some inherited problems. As mentioned, some families may tend to be more animal aggressive than others. This trait, which was highly desired during the "pit" days, must still be considered as an inherited condition. This, and other isolated family traits and inheritances, would almost be from strain to strain rather than representa-

tive of these breeds as a whole. Your breeder-mentor would be the best source of information about inherited traits and behaviors, good or bad, in the ancestry of the puppy that you choose.

Parasites

Internal Parasites

Roundworms: Roundworms can infest dogs of all ages even though puppies are most often the victims of this internal pest. The pups often have roundworms even before they are born, having gotten them from their mother prenatally.

Roundworms will sap the vigor and growth potential of little terrier pups. They siphon off a puppy's bright and shiny look and pull down its vitality. Youngsters simply cannot thrive when anchored down by these parasites.

Your veterinarian can rid your pups and their mother of these health robbers. You may discover roundworms in your pup's stool or vomitus. Seek immediate professional treatment.

Because good kennel hygiene can cut down on roundworm infestations, keep any areas the puppies share especially clean and sanitary. Get rid of stools quickly and appropriately and pay close attention to kennel and home cleanliness. The larval forms of this parasite are transmissible to humans.

Hookworms: Hookworms, like roundworms, can be in evidence in dogs throughout their lives. Hookworms are also especially hard on puppies, who simply will not thrive while these worms are in them. Puppies with hookworms will have bloody stools or their feces will appear very dark and tarlike.

Hookworms are little bloodsuckers that attach themselves to the insides of a puppy's small intestines. Pups with hookworms will sometimes become anemic, and these parasites reduce a puppy's ability to fight off disease. As with all internal parasites, your veterinarian is the sworn enemy of hookworms and will dispatch them for the good of your puppy.

Tapeworms: Tapeworms are a parasite brought by a parasite. Fleas are the host of tapeworms and when your dog has fleas, it can also have tapeworms. Your Amstaff or APBT will never be at its best while infested with tapeworms. Keep fleas off your dog and out of its environment and then get tapeworms out of your dog.

Your veterinarian will be able to help you dispose of both parasitic problems—the fleas and the tapeworms. Because tapeworms can really hamper a puppy's growth and a dog's potential, get them and any other internal parasites treated as soon as possible.

Heartworms: The heartworm is another parasite that comes to you compliments of a pest. Heartworms are transmitted to your pet through infested mosquitoes. The mosquito bites your pet and deposits heartworm larvae on your dog. These larvae enter the dog's bloodstream through the mosquito bite. Once in the dog's bloodstream, the larvae will ultimately make their way to the dog's heart. Once there, they will grow and increasingly clog this crucial organ until your pet is fatally affected.

Heartworms have expanded their territory thanks to their mosquito hosts. Today a large part of the United States is threatened by heartworm infestation. The diagnosis for heartworms is made using a blood test. Your veterinarian will help you devise a plan to prevent heartworms from infesting your APBT or Amstaff or in treating an affected animal. The preventive plan will involve regular preventive testing and regular doses of preventive medicine that will kill heartworm larvae before they can enter the dog's heart.

Mosquitoes spread heartworm larvae from infected dogs to healthy dogs. These larvae can mature in a dog's heart and cause great, often fatal, damage.

Dogs with heartworms can be treated, but this is a risky, long, and expensive procedure. Prevention of heartworm problems is best for you and best for your dog!

External Parasites

Fleas: Fleas are the curse of many dogs' lives. They are the most common parasite affecting dogs and they literally feed on your dog's blood. In very severe infestations, fleas can cause anemic conditions in canines, and anemia could lead to death especially in puppies. Fleas add insult to injury in that they are also the host and introducer of tapeworms into dogs.

Some dogs, like some humans, can have a severe allergic reaction to these pests. This flea-bite allergy can cause severe scratching, hair loss, and absolute misery to the afflicted dog. This condition requires immediate treatment by a veterinarian to diagnose and treat the allergy. The owner will have to be absolutely fanatical about ridding the dog's living area of all fleas.

Dealing with fleas involves a "take no prisoners" mentality. The sooner you understand that fleas are your and your dog's mortal enemy and take charge of an eradication program, the sooner your pet will be safe from fleas. If your dog has fleas, there will be fleas *everywhere* your dog can go. This will include your home, your yard, your car, the dog's kennel area, and so forth. If you fail to rid any of these places of all the fleas, eggs, and pupae that exist, you have failed in all the places—for the fleas will soon be back.

Consult with your veterinarian and with a knowledgeable pet products person to discover the weapons at your disposal to wipe fleas from the face of your dog's world. Flea dips, shampoos, collars, dusts, and sprays are on-dog weapons. Foggers, carpet cleaners, and in-home sprays take care of the dwelling. Yard sprays and kennel dust will stop the fleas that lie in wait outside the home. Be sure to remember to treat those places where the dog may only go sometimes: the car, or the cottage at the lake.

Fleas spend 90 percent of their life cycle *off* your dog. Only the adult fleas, about 10 percent of the flea population, are actually on your pet. Deal with the 90 percent either by using products designed for each area (always use great care and always follow the directions!). Your regular exterminator may also be able to help in large areas like your home and yard.

Ticks: Ticks are usually much larger than fleas and they can siphon off just that much more blood. Ticks will fill up on your dog's blood and will grow several times their original size. Their bites on a short-haired dog like the APBT and Amstaff can become unsightly scars. Tick bites also can become infected.

Ticks are not only a general nuisance; they can carry the life-threatening Lyme disease (see Borelliosis, page 85) and other diseases, such as Rocky Mountain spotted fever, that can affect dogs and humans. Ticks can readily move from your dog, to your children, or to you.

Fortunately, ticks don't seem to be the tough foe that fleas are. They can usually be controlled by the regular use of veterinary-recommended sprays, dips, powders, and flea and tick collars for on-dog use. You may also want to treat the living area with an anti-tick spray that will keep them from getting back on your pet later.

Ear mites: Your Amstaff or American pit bull terrier's ears can become the target of another external parasite, the bothersome ear mite. These microscopic little pests live both in the ear and in the ear canal. You can spot their presence there by a dirty, waxy, dark residue on the skin inside the ear.

Ear mites can cause your dog a lot of discomfort. If you see your pet shaking its head from side to side in a violent manner, or if your dog constantly digs at or scratches at its ears, ear mites are possibly to blame.

Although there are home remedies that can stop these mites, always follow your veterinarian's preferred method of handling these parasites. As you look for ticks in your American Staffordshire terrier's or APBT's ears, look for evidence of ear mites.

Mange: There are two kinds of mange, both of which are caused by a mite:
• Demodectic, or red, mange especially affects puppies and old dogs. Both of these ages are especially susceptible to the ragged and patchy appearance, especially around the head and face, that is commonly called

Safely Removing a Tick from Your Dog

• Never simply pull a tick off your APBT/Amstaff. Doing so may leave part of the tick in your dog's skin, which cannot only be irritating, but which could lead to a bad infection or even a bad scar.

• Place a small amount of rubbing alcohol precisely at the site of the tick's mouth and bite. Make sure that the alcohol doesn't get into your dog's eyes or mouth!

• With the dog being held or remaining still, carefully use tweezers to grasp the tick as close as possible to the dog's skin. *Very slowly* pull out the tick's mouth and head from the bite it made in your dog.

• Be certain to carefully get any tick mouth parts out of the bite. When you think you have removed all of the tick, put a little alcohol on the bite or use another antiseptic to help prevent infection.

• When using the tweezers, be very careful that you don't do more damage to the dog than a tick bite. If a tick is deep in your pet's ear or very near an eye, you would be well advised to let your veterinarian handle this tick removal.

• After a tick is removed, don't just drop it on the ground. Ticks can get back on a dog or another blood source. Dispose of the tick in a proper fashion. Because of the deer tick potential as a Lyme disease carrier, you should have all ticks positively identified.

• Sometimes you will see *two* ticks at one bite site. The larger of the two will be female, and she will be blood engorged. The smaller tick will be the male. Be sure to carefully get all of both ticks out of your dog's skin.

• Make regular inspections of your dog, especially on the shoulders, head, and ears after you have been in any environment where ticks may be able to get on your pet.

• Consider having your backyard or kennel area regularly sprayed with a veterinarian-approved product to reduce tick infestations.

• Prior to going for walks or hikes in areas where ticks may be lurking, spray some flea and tick spray on your pet to reduce the chances of bringing some of these parasites home with you.

To remove a tick, place a drop of alcohol at the bite site. Slowly pull out all of the tick and dispose of it in a jar of alcohol or gasoline.

mangy. Red mange usually causes patchy hair loss around the eyes and face. Occasionally it can cause severe hair loss and severe itching.

• Sarcoptic mange also is caused by a mite. This one burrows into your dog's skin. It usually causes significant hair loss and intense scratching that can make unsightly raw wounds on a dog's skin, which can become infected. Sarcoptic mange mites can also live temporarily on humans, causing an itchy rash.

Your veterinarian can provide a treatment plan for both kinds of mange and keep your pet from the ugly, uncomfortable, and unhealthy side effects of these tiny mites.

HOW-TO:
Helping an Injured Pet

- Remain calm yourself. Your pet will pick up on your anxiety if you let it show.
- Speak to the pet in a calm, confident voice to reassure it that you are here to take the hurt away. Your dog will usually have confidence in you that you can make things all right.
- Move very slowly, with no sudden moves that could alarm an injured and frightened animal.
- Even if this dog is your lifelong pal, muzzle it gently, but securely. An APBT- or Amstaff-sized muzzle might be a good investment just in case of injuries, but a necktie, leash, or belt might also work.
- After the dog is muzzled, immediately attend to any bleeding (see Bleeding, page 93).
- Be very supportive when you try to move an adult American Staffordshire or American pit bull terrier. If you can get someone else to help you, certainly do so. If you can get something, such as a door or wide

An improvised stretcher can be used to help move an injured pet without making matters worse.

board, to serve as a safe and secure stretcher, use it.
- If you are alone, you may have to use your coat, a piece of carpet, or a tarp to devise a way for you to safely move the pet, gently sliding the dog along if you cannot, or if it is not advisable to lift it.
- Call your veterinarian, or have someone else do it, to

alert the clinic of the injury and of your arrival time.
- Drive *safely* to the veterinarian. You are more likely to make things worse by driving like a madman.
- Follow the age-old medical precept of "First, do no harm" in all of your actions designed to help an injured pet!

Making a muzzle out of a leash, belt, or necktie may keep an injured dog from injuring itself further of from hurting someone else.

Emergency Care for Your APBT/Amstaff

Accidents

Hopefully you will have done everything you can to prevent accidents, but even the best dog owner cannot anticipate every situation where an accident could occur. Even if you can't really anticipate, you can be really prepared!

The primary rule in trying to help an injured pet is *don't make things worse!* You could get bitten yourself if you carelessly approach even a trusted pet who is confused, in pain, and frightened. If you are injured, that will delay the help you need to get for your dog. Your first step is to find some way to muzzle and immobilize your pet so that it won't hurt you or itself.

Don't be in too much of a rush to move a nonmoving pet. Rough treatment can cause a relatively minor injury to become a severe or even fatal injury. Think clearly and remember that you are your pet's best hope only if you are acting rationally.

If your Amstaff or American pit bull terrier is involved in a fight, remember that these breeds are more likely to make use of their powerful jaws to grab on, hold on, and shake the opponent. If the other dog is some breed other than an Amstaff or an APBT, you are more likely to be bitten by it, as you try to separate them, than by yours.

Heatstroke

The most ludicrous way for a dog to die in the entire world is for its owner to leave it in a parked car on a day when the outside temperature is 60°F (15.6°C). The metal of the car and the heat-increasing properties of auto glass can turn the family sedan into an oven of death for a pet left there for even a few minutes!

Clinical signs of heatstroke include a dazed look and rapid, shallow panting with a high fever. The dog's gums will be bright red.

Speed is crucial if a dog is in this condition. Act *immediately*. Lower your pet's temperature by pouring a mixture of cool water and rubbing alcohol all over the dog's body, then transport your pet to the nearest veterinarian!

Bleeding

The first thing to do when a dog is bleeding is to correctly identify the source of the bleeding. After you are sure that you have the source and not just a bloody spot, apply firm, but gentle, pressure to the wound with your hand. If the wound is on an extremity (front legs, back legs, tail), place a tourniquet between the injury and the dog's heart. Loosen the tourniquet for 30 to 60 seconds every 15 minutes. If the bleeding continues, or if there is significant blood loss, or if it is a gaping wound, your veterinarian should be consulted as soon as possible!

Recognizing Potential Poisons

Your American pit bull terrier or American Staffordshire terrier can be hurt in many ways, but one of the greatest places of risk is right in your

After securely muzzling a pet with a bleeding wound, apply a tourniquet between the wound and the heart and promptly seek veterinarian care.

Cleaning your dog's teeth on a regular basis will help prevent plaque buildup and tooth decay.

home. There are in our modern society many opportunities for a pet to ingest some drug or chemical that could end its life.

• Antifreeze is deadly to dogs and it has a sweet taste that attracts them. Spilled or leaked antifreeze can be difficult to spot, but your pet can find it.

• Chocolate, almost an addiction in many homes, can kill a dog or puppy if eaten in sufficient quantity.

• A number of yard and garden plants are dangerous to pets, especially to young pups that enjoy chewing on things. Favorites such as azalea, rhododendron, and holly, can bring death to a young dog. Wild plants like mistletoe and poison ivy can cause severe, even fatal, reactions in some dogs. Check with your local county extension service for a list of poisonous plants that thrive where you live.

• Houseplants like dieffenbachia, poinsettia, and jade plants can all be killers. Ask your extension service about a list of local favorites and check out any houseplant's poison potential before you bring it into your home.

• Common household chemicals can take the life of an inquisitive dog.

Keep all insecticides, pesticides, garden and lawn chemicals, and cleaning solvents away from places your Amstaff or APBT can prowl.

If your dog suddenly becomes listless, convulses, seems disoriented, or is unconscious, it may be a poison victim. Other signs of poison ingestion include a change in color of the mucous membranes, vomiting, and diarrhea. The presence of these signs is worth a trip to the veterinarian that may save the life of your pet!

Areas Requiring Lifelong Attention

Teeth

Your APBT or Amstaff will depend greatly on its teeth all its life. These dogs put even greater pressure on their teeth than do most other breeds. Unless you pay close attention to your dog's "choppers" beginning when it is a very young puppy, teeth problems could become a source of pain, discomfort, unpleasant breath, or even life-threatening infections. Dental care for dogs can't just be turned over to your veterinarian during your twice-yearly, regular visits. As with humans, the care of your Amstaff or APBT's mouth, gums, and teeth should be a daily activity between you and your pet.

Caring for Your Dog's Teeth

• Regular inspections will alert you to any abnormalities. Everyday, as you pet or play with your American pit bull terrier or American Staffordshire terrier, take just a moment to settle the pet down to look at its mouth.

• Look at the teeth, gums, throat, and lips not just for tooth decay, but for the presence of tartar and foreign objects (like pieces of wood or bone from the dog's chewing habits).

• Pay attention to tartar as it can bring on gum disease and tooth decay. It also makes the dog's mouth look bad.

• Start very early with the Amstaff or APBT puppy to clean its teeth. As with so many other areas of dog ownership, the earlier you start it, the easier it will be!

• To clean your pet's teeth, use veterinarian-approved brushes and utensils and a toothpaste designed for dogs not humans! Canine teeth cleaning is not difficult if you can get the pet to come to enjoy or accept it early. Teeth cleaning will also largely involve brushing if you begin the practice with a puppy and continue it often and regularly, two or three times a week, with daily brushing being even better.

• Tartar scraping is never pleasant and comes as a result of neglecting your dog's teeth for too long a period. This severe tartar removal may have to be done at the veterinarian's.

• Schedule regular veterinary dental checkups with occasional professional teeth cleaning to catch any areas you may have missed.

• Use veterinarian-approved and experienced Amstaff/APBT breeder-reviewed chew toys and dental exercisers to help in keeping tartar at a minimum.

Note: Remember that chew toys and other similar items designed for the average dog may *not* be adequate for your American pit bull terrier or American Staffordshire terrier that has the most powerful jaws in dogdom! If your APBT demolishes inappropriate chewing devices, pieces could be swallowed and necessitate surgery to remove them from the dog's intestines.

• The only adequate way to clean your pet's teeth is through regular care by you and regular cleaning by a professional. Dog biscuits, chew toys, and rawhide strips are no substitute for good home care and professional attention.

Eyes

Your American pit bull terrier or American Staffordshire terrier does not have the large prominent eyes of some breeds. This fact does not mean that these dogs will be immune to eye injuries or eye problems. Often dogs of these breeds are very exuberant and active. Such "love of life" can cause a pet to not notice possible eye-injuring situations. As the pet owner, it will be your job to help prevent these injuries. There are several ways to do this:

• In places where your pet is allowed to play or run, be alert for sharp pointed things the dog might not see, like thorns, briars, barbed wire, stems, and rosebushes (especially those that may have been recently trimmed and are just at a dog's eye level).

• Caution children about throwing stones, playing with air rifles, and other activities that could be injurious to a curious pet's eyes.

• Keep your pet from chemical harm to its eyes by avoiding places where considerable air pollution is taking place or where recent or residual chemical spraying could be on grass or shrubs and get into your pet's eyes.

• Don't let your pet ride with its head out of a automobile window.

• Check your dog's eyes every day for injuries, foreign matter, reddening, or infection. You may notice that mucus sometimes appears in the corners of your American Staffordshire or APBT's eyes. Normally, this is perfectly natural and can simply be removed gently with a soft cloth. This mucus should not be confused with a discharge that needs veterinary attention.

Ears

Your American pit bull terrier or American Staffordshire terrier can have either cropped ears (see the UKC and AKC breed standards, pages 15 and 16) or uncropped or "natural" ears. Although it is admittedly more

Keep you dog's nails trimmed using a guillotine-style nail trimmer. The inset shows the correct direction in which to file the nails, avoiding the "quick," or vein, which should not be cut.

difficult for an uncropped show dog to win against cropped dogs, it does happen.

Cropping for American pit bull terriers and American Staffordshire terriers is very different from the ear surgery performed on Great Danes, Dobermans, and some others. Originally a protection against ear injuries in the pit, the medium-length crop now used on Amstaffs and APBTs is not as short as its pit predecessors, but not nearly as long as that of the Dane and Dobe.

Cropping is largely a matter of personal preference. This cosmetic surgery is usually done by a veterinarian when the puppy is a couple of months old. Not every veterinary practitioner will want to, or will even know how to, do this for the style that fits current show preferences. Discuss with your breed mentor and other APBT or Amstaff breeders whom they would recommend.

Cropped or uncropped ears will still need daily inspection for injuries,

infection, or infestations of ear mites or ticks (see page 90). Pay attention to the inside and the outside of the dog's ears. Keep young children from biting, pulling, or hitting a dog's ears and don't let sticks or toys become ear harmers.

Feet and Toenails

Your American pit bull terrier or American Staffordshire terrier usually has sturdy feet, well able to support a sturdy medium-sized dog, but every dog can sometimes have trouble down where the "dog meets the ground."

If your dog lives with you in an urban setting, there are both good and bad aspects to what city life can do to a dog's feet. It is true that running over paved surfaces can keep the toenails worn down where they may not need much trimming. It is also true that city-dwelling APBTs and Amstaffs will suffer more damage to the pads of their feet from the rough unyielding surfaces of concrete, paving stone, and asphalt. Bruises and abrasions are more often seen in this environment. Salt on winter sidewalks can also be an irritant to dog feet.

The rural APBT or Amstaff won't miss out on foot concerns either. Constantly walking or running in a grassy backyard will not wear down nails and these will grow too long unless you trim them. Splinters, thorns, slivers of broken glass, and even small stones can get between a pet's toes or in the soft tissue of the pad and cause trouble.

Daily inspections of your dog's feet will prevent most minor conditions or small hurts from becoming major problems. Trimming your dog's toenails, like brushing its teeth, must be started early to be easily accomplished. You need a good set of canine nail clippers. These can be either the scissors type or the "guillotine" type. As your dog's nails grow, trim back just the

Neither healthy, happy children nor puppies just happen. They both need consistent care, training, and love.

tips on each nail (see the illustration). Don't cut too deeply or the "quick," or blood supply to the nail, will be injured and may bleed. Following trimming, smooth the edges of the nail with a nail file or an emery board

Giving Your APBT/Amstaff Medicine

You should know how to administer the prescriptions your veterinarian gives you to keep your pet healthy or help it regain its health. This activity is not always as easy as it sounds, and like a lot of American pit bull terrier or American Staffordshire terrier care, it should start in puppyhood.

Some dogs just don't like to be dosed with medicine. They will spit out capsules or tablets. Some dog owners will hide a pill in a treat in order to get it down.

A more direct approach and one that can be used when a dog may catch on to the treat trick is to:
1. Speak calmly and reassuringly as you open the dog's mouth.

2. Tilt its head back only slightly.
3. Place the pill as far back on the dog's tongue as possible (or in the case of liquid medicine, pour it over the back of the tongue).
4. Gently but firmly close the dog's mouth, holding the jaws closed with your hand, and continue to talk to the dog until it swallows the medicine.

Always remember to follow the veterinarian's instructions, dosages, and medication schedule carefully. Never give your American pit bull terrier or Amstaff human medicines or remedies without your veterinarian's prior approval.

When Your APBT/Amstaff Grows Older

These breeds have a good, long life span and may be with you and your family up into the teens of years. Gradually that humorous, innocent puppy that became that powerful American pit bull terrier or American Staffordshire terrier will turn into a gray-muzzled senior. Normally, a dog of these breeds will age well and keep both its good health and its devotion to its humans.

The oldster will sleep a little more, play a little less. It will still want to be included in family activities and not be replaced by a younger and more vigorous puppy. All of the teeth, eyes, ears, and feet and toenail care take on added importance with a distinguished veteran. Your visits to the veterinarian may come a little more often as your pet's health needs change.

You will need to be certain that the dog is fed a good "senior" dog food that will not contribute to obesity, a condition that will really hurt an older pet. Your pet may need a little less food and a few more frequent walks and visits to the relief spot.

All in all, the magic of the American pit bull terrier or the American Staffordshire terrier will still be there. Slower, more willing to watch than participate, but still desperately in need of your loving touch and approval, your older pet will still have as much affection for you and your family as it ever had. You will need to be sure that your old dog knows that you still love it too.

Saying Good-bye (Euthanasia)

That inquisitive, little Amstaff or APBT that won your heart at the breeder's will make way for the frisky adolescent and then the sturdy adult. Over the years, this American Staffordshire or American pit bull ter-

rier will have become a trusted and greatly loved member of your family.

One day your APBT/Amstaff may begin a downward slide in health and activity. Under ideal circumstances, your pet would be relatively healthy one day, and then quietly, and painlessly die in its sleep that night. Such ease in a negative situation would be a blessing that rarely mirrors reality.

In most cases, barring fatal accidents or injuries, an old dog will just grow older and older until age and infirmity makes its existence one of pain and anguish. It is at this point that the hardest decision a pet owner will ever have to make must be made.

When the life of your loving American Staffordshire or American pit bull terrier becomes void of the fun of former times and when the dog looks to you with imploring eyes for an explanation for all the pain and physical incapacity, your decision must be one based on the best interests of the dog.

Your veterinarian and your breed-mentor, now hopefully old friends to both you and your American Staffordshire terrier or APBT, can be consulted. Euthanasia will be a gentle end to a full and happy life that has taken on very painful aspects. Ultimately the decision is yours and it will never be easy, but there comes a time when you grasp all the positive memories and hold them tight and say good-bye to a dear and devoted friend.

Breeding and Raising APBT/Amstaff Terriers

The Decision—to Breed or not to Breed

The decision as to whether you should attempt to breed and raise American Staffordshire or American pit bull terriers should never be hurriedly or casually decided. Even more important, it should *never* be solely left up to the hormonal impulses of your dog! Don't let a bitch in heat or a male in search of one get you into dog breeding. If your dog is not spayed or neutered, it should be securely fenced, kept in a kennel, or staying inside your home when natural reproductive urges could produce an unwanted litter of puppies.

Before you decide that you want to allow more American pit bull terriers or American Staffordshire terriers to be born, give these aspects some thought:
• There are many more dogs, pure-bred and otherwise, than there are good homes for them.
• Each puppy that you allow your dog to produce should have a reasonable expectation of a happy life.
• There is no money in dog breeding. Other than some factory breeders and some very successful show or field trial breeders, most people who are involved with dogs *spend* money much faster than they make it!
• The only legitimate reason to produce more American pit bull terrier or Amstaff puppies is to improve the breed. Unless a mating has a better than even chance of doing this, that mating shouldn't take place.
• When your APBT or Amstaff bitch produces a litter, you will then be responsible for finding good homes for *all* that litter. If you can't place each one, how many are you prepared to have live with you for the rest of their lives?
• Your chance of producing even one excellent show prospect are remote. Breeders who have been raising Amstaffs/APBTs for years feel lucky when they produce even one top puppy out of a litter. The top puppies are easy to find homes for, but what about the rest of its littermates?
• Raising healthy puppies will be a labor-intensive task that may require quite a bit of time, money, and effort.

Key Questions to Ask Yourself

Before you decide to breed your APBT/Amstaff, honestly answer these key questions:

1. Am I motivated enough to find the best possible American Staffordshire or American pit bull with which to start?
2. Am I and my family willing to commit the necessary resources, financial and other, to this possibly risky endeavor?
3. Am I willing to really search for the best possible homes for all the American pit bull terrier or Amstaff puppies I raise?
4. Am I willing to maintain a lifelong interest in the care of any dogs I allow to be born, even if I have to keep several of them in my own home?
5. Do I and my family have the time and the willingness to help each puppy become effectively socialized?

By following the mother dog's pattern of training puppies, you will find training your puppy to be much easier and much more effective.

6. Am I interested in breeding American Staffordshires or American pit bull terriers in order to produce the absolutely best possible puppies?

7. Am I willing to accept the opinion of dog show judges and other breeders if they find that my Amstaff or APBT is not of sufficient quality to use as breeding stock or that any puppies produced in my breedings are not show quality?

8. Am I willing to accept the fact that some people are going to judge any dog I own or raise not by its own merits but by its breed name or the breed grouping into which it falls?

9. Am I willing to spend a lot of time reading, studying, and asking questions of experts about pedigrees, strains, or families in order to become an adequate breeder?

10. Am I willing to spay or neuter my pet if it is not breeding stock quality and am I willing to enforce this spay/neuter policy on any purchaser of a pet-quality puppy that I may raise?

Set Your APBT/Amstaff Goals High

You will discover that there are a good many sources for dogs. Some of these dogs will be registered in one or more registries and yet be far from what you want to even own, much less want to own for breeding purposes!

If you have serious aspirations to breed dogs, especially American Staffordshire terriers or American pit bull terriers, you will need to obtain the best puppy possible. This may require thousands of miles of traveling and thousands of dollars in expenses, even before you consider the cost of the right pup. If you want to breed dogs, bypass all the purely profit-centered people and other irresponsible breeders. Go for the very best. Study and find what may be the top Amstaff or APBT puppy born in the United States this year and invest what it will take to buy it.

If you own such a puppy, show this puppy to its championship in whatever registry it may belong (both UKC *and* AKC championships would be icing on the cake!). Have your pup's breeding potential evaluated by experienced APBT/Amstaff breeders and knowledgeable judges. Weigh their opinions carefully. Recognize that many great show dogs will not produce offspring as good as they are, even when bred to other great show dogs.

Breeding dogs is not unlike putting together one of those big jigsaw puzzles, except that you are doing it in the dark! The producing of top-quality dogs requires that you put together dogs that have genetic characteristics that are compatible with each other. Because there may be several hundred or more characteristics and because most of these are not visible, you are trying to fit pieces together only by the way these pieces have appeared in your dog and its ancestry and the chosen mate and its ancestry.

The old stock breeder's credo of "like produces like" is true as far as it goes. Your dog, if bred to another dog, will produce a dog. Your APBT or Amstaff, bred to another APBT or Amstaff, will produce an APBT or an Amstaff. Where this old adage doesn't work is in the multitude of fine points that fill each breed's standard and in the even greater multitude of fine points that fill each dog's DNA (deoxyribonucleic acid) or genetic signature.

Another old saying is that "water seeks its own level." This is the far truer of the two statements. You can breed the two best dogs in a breed and you may, if you get lucky, get one pup as good as its parents. Some breeders may get very lucky and have two, three, or four puppies of exceptional quality. This may happen only rarely to even the best of breeders.

If you breed a genetically superior dog to a dog of lesser genetic quality, the lesser dog will invariably pull down the superior dog's influence in the offspring. In breeding animals, the backgrounds or pedigrees are about as

important as the visible impact of the animal itself. If a particular quality, for example, good temperament, isn't present in the parents or in the parents' parents, it would be miraculous if it were to be present in the offspring!

Start with the very best if you decide to try breeding American Staffordshire terriers or American pit bull terriers. If you don't aim high, you will be far, far better off to never breed your dog. If you want a top American Staffordshire terrier or American pit bull terrier show puppy each year, you will save much money and even more time by going out and *buying* it instead of trying to *breed* it.

The Dam (Mother Dog)

Temperament, Condition, Quality, Compatibility

There are four building blocks that you *must* consider when deciding to breed your American pit bull terrier or American Staffordshire terrier bitch. Without excellence in all four of these, your female should be kept as the family pet and left out of the breeding pen.

Temperament: Important in every breed, essential in APBTs and Amstaffs, temperament must be a number one consideration. Without a good disposition around other dogs and around strangers, your dog is a pretty unpredictable pet. Such a pet should certainly not be allowed to reproduce!

Condition: Before a bitch should be considered as possible breeding stock, she should be evaluated by your veterinarian to see that she is in good health. In order to not only withstand the rigors of producing and raising a litter of puppies, but to produce and raise a litter of *healthy* puppies, your bitch will need to be in top condition.

She can't be too fat or too thin. She can't be just getting over a major illness that will require her health reserves. She can't be too young. She can't be too old.

Quality: As discussed (see Pet Quality or Show Quality, page 31), quality has nothing to do with your female's good points as a companion dog and member of your family. If her temperament and her condition are good enough, the next barrier to cross is her fitness as an Amstaff or American pit bull terrier. Simply, is she an AKC champion American Staffordshire terrier or a UKC champion American pit bull terrier? Campaigning her under several breed judges through enough shows for her to win her championship *may* be a good indicator that she should be considered for breeding. Unless some injury or nongenetic flaw has kept your female from pursuing a championship, she probably won't produce top-quality show puppies.

An added benefit to defining her quality would be if she also has an obedience title behind her name along with her show championship. These two facts would make most breeders fairly sure that she could be a potential breeder, as your female would be an excellent specimen of the breed and possess excellent trainability.

Compatibility: The final building block for your APBT or Amstaff's breeding credentials is her projected genetic compatibility with a particular possible stud dog. One way to evaluate potential is to see what kind of puppies the relatives of your dog have produced either with this potential stud choice himself or with his relatives. If your bitch's sister produced excellent puppies when bred to this dog, or to his father, or to his brother, this may be a pretty good possible mating. If your bitch's father sired top-quality puppies when mated with the potential sire's female relatives, it is also possible this mating may be a good one.

The Sire (Father Dog)

It is highly unlikely that you would have been able to obtain an Amstaff or American pit bull terrier male puppy as your first dog of these breeds and it would become a superior stud dog. Not even every show champion will become a good stud dog and you are not looking for merely a good stud dog. If you are going to the trouble and expense to breed your APBT or American Staffordshire terrier bitch, by all means breed her to the best dog in the country that fits her pedigree. Certainly you will want to use the top stud in your part of the country. Don't chicken out or cheapen out when it comes to finding the right male to sire your good-quality bitch's puppies.

Temperament, Condition, Quality, Compatibility

Temperament: As with your female, the male chosen to sire her pups must be nothing less than superb in temperament. Some breeders rank the temperament of the male in importance over that of even the mother dog. The male generally has more opportunities to act up and show his true temperament than do some females. Go with nothing but the best in this important aspect!

Condition: Although important, the overall immediate health of the sire is not as crucial as the condition of the female that will carry and raise the pups. Of course, he can't be in bad physical condition or he may not be able to successfully mate, but it is important that this male be in excellent genetic condition and that he has shown a history of imbuing his offspring with this good genetic heritage. If your choice of stud dogs brings a bad record where the puppies he has sired have not been healthy, no matter how good he is in *all* the other areas, skip this dog!

Quality: Unless an American pit bull terrier or American Staffordshire terrier is an exceptional specimen, an AKC/UKC champion with possibly an obedience title also, he's probably not the sire you're seeking. As stated, you have searched and found the best possible female puppy. You have cared for her, nurtured her, and trained her. She has been evaluated and found to be of sufficient quality herself to merit being considered for breeding purposes. Don't waste her time and health, or your time and money, by breeding her to anything but an absolutely exceptional male.

Compatibility: As discussed with the brood bitch, the compatibility aspect of your dog with the selected stud is of crucial importance to your breeding effort. If you have the top American pit bull terrier or American Staffordshire terrier female in the country, and you chose the top male American pit bull terrier or American Staffordshire terrier and they don't have genetic compatibility, you may produce a litter of really nice, pet-quality puppies with some great names in their pedigrees. Without compatibility, you have only two really good-looking dogs and that may be as far as it goes!

Sires are often judged by their "prepotency." This means that they are able to produce puppies as good as they themselves are even when bred to females not quite as good. A prepotent stud is highly sought after by the owners of top-quality bitches because of the potential such a stud dog has of producing the next great, prepotent stud or perhaps the mother of the next great prepotent stud.

Always depend on your experienced Amstaff or APBT breeder friends when deciding on a sire. They will have been immersed in breed pedigrees, puppy records, prepotency, compatibility, and all the other jargon of the serious dog breeder. They will also have an idea about which male will fit with your female and they may be right.

Breeding your American pit bull terrier or Amstaff bitch to a top stud dog will probably be expensive. Stud fees vary, sometimes including a set monetary fee, or a pick-of-the-litter puppy, or both. This picked puppy will be the stud owner's choice, not yours.

The owner of a prominent stud dog may require a written certificate that your bitch has no obvious congenital or physical conditions and that she is free of the venerally transmitted bacterial disease of canine brucellosis. Canine brucellosis is incurable and may possibly be transmitted to humans. It can cause great harm to breeding dogs, causing sterility in males and aborted litters in females.

The stud dog's owner will want to be very certain that your bitch will not bring harm to the stud. This concern will not only be about such diseases as brucellosis, but as to whether your bitch may try to fight with the stud at mating time and possibly injure him. The area of harm to the reputation of a top stud is also foremost in the minds of some male dog owners.

If your bitch is mated to a top stud and produces a litter of several genetically deformed puppies, or puppies that look like they could have been sired by a male of another breed, the reputation of this stud may suffer. Because top studs can make money from stud fees, no owner will want to breed to a poor-quality female. The better the puppies the stud produces, the more his services will be sought.

The stud owner should offer you a guarantee that the mating will result in conception and with some living puppies. Normally, if your bitch does not become pregnant or "misses," the stud's owner will allow a rebreeding at the bitch's next heat. This is usually offered in writing.

When Should You Breed Your APBT/Amstaff Female?

Age

It is generally considered best that your female be at least two years old and have received her OFA evaluation before she is bred. This will also give her time to show the kind of female she is in the show ring or in obedience.

The Estrous Cycle

Your American Staffordshire terrier or American pit bull terrier bitch will usually come into season, or heat, twice a year. Her first heat will probably occur between the ages of six and eight months of age (although some females mature faster than others). Just the presence of her first heat does *not* indicate that she should be allowed to have puppies. It is merely her first estrous cycle that can have several phases and several outcomes.

The stages of the estrous cycle are: proestrus, estrus, metestrus, and anestrus. Each stage has its own purpose and its own signs and all are part of the reproductive life of a female dog.

Proestrus: Proestrus is the first stage of the cycle. It is identified by the beginnings of activity within the uterus and the ovaries. The ovaries start to produce eggs, or ova. As these ova mature, the uterus wall become thicker, the external genitalia (the vulva) gets larger, and a blood-tinged discharge from the bitch's vagina will be observable.

Proestrus will last about nine days, although it can be as short as four or as long as 14 days. During proestrus, males will be attracted to your Amstaff/APBT female, but she will not be ready to mate with them.

Estrus: Estrus is the next phase of the estrous cycle. Now the vaginal discharge will become clearer and thicker. Ovulation actually takes place during the estrus stage, usually

between the ninth and fourteenth days following the onset of the estrous cycle. Mating and conception can occur during estrus, which may last as long as nine days.

Metestrus: If your American pit bull terrier or Amstaff bitch mated and conceived during estrus, her reproductive organs will now begin to adapt for the birth of the puppies. The onset of metestrus will bring the beginning of mammary growth and preparation for lactation (milk production).

Anestrus: Anestrus signals the end of metestrus and with it the completion of the estrous cycle. In anestrus, the uterus and the ovaries will begin changing back to their pre-estrous cycle appearance. If your female did not mate and conceive, her organs will gradually return to normal. There will be a cessation of vaginal discharge. Her ovaries will become inactive. She will be in a form of "reproductive shutdown" until her body signals the start of heat or the estrous cycle all over again in about six months time.

Note: During the entire estrous cycle, commonly referred to as heat or in season, your female APBT/Amstaff should be kept away from breeding-age males (including older male pups). You should make every effort to protect her during this time from an unwanted pregnancy.

Mating

The stud dog is normally allowed access to the female on the ninth day of the ovulating part of the cycle or the estrus stage. When dogs mate, the male and the female usually become "tied" when the male's enlarged penis is in effect locked within the female's vagina. This "tied" condition should last only a few minutes.

If the male and female remain together or are reintroduced again during approximately two days of the female's maximum time of receptiveness, they may mate again, but this second mating is not usually needed to insure conception.

Note: Control of your American pit bull terrier or American Staffordshire terrier bitch during the entire mating time is very important. Just because she has mated once with the stud dog of your choice does not mean that she cannot mate again with another APBT/Amstaff or even with a dog of another breed. If she is allowed to mate with a second dog, the parentage of her puppies could be called into question. Most registries will disallow any puppies born when two males mate with the same bitch during a single estrus.

Pregnancy

If your American Staffordshire terrier or American pit bull terrier bitch has mated with the stud you selected and subsequently conceived, her puppies will normally be born between 58 and 63 days after the mating. During this waiting period, known as gestation, your female will begin to take on the appearance of pregnancy. Her teats will become larger in preparation for feeding hungry, APBT/Amstaff newborns. Her abdomen will gradually become fuller and may balloon out or sag a bit.

Special Diet

During gestation, your soon-to-be-mother dog will need some extra care. She will need some high-quality food, preferably a puppy food during the last third of her pregnancy and on through lactation and weaning. This will give her the nutrition she needs to produce the puppies and also maintain her own health. It is important to remember that the bitch needs to be heavy with her developing litter and not heavy with excess fat. Fat mother dogs will have greater difficulty producing and then birthing puppies.

Moderate exercise is advised, until about two weeks before the puppies are due. At this time, it would be wise to eliminate any strenuous activity from her lifestyle. Separate her from other dogs and keep her as comfortable and stress-free as possible during the final days before the puppies arrive.

TLC (Tender Loving Care)

Especially if this is her first litter, you should take extra care with your APBT/Amstaff female. She will not understand all that is happening to her and she may need added reassurance from you. Your extra attention will help to convey to her that what is happening is all right.

The Whelping Box

You should make every effort to be prepared for the upcoming birth of the puppies. One of the best and most necessary things you can do is to construct a whelping (birth) box. This box can be constructed of plywood and finished lumber or is available in a prefab model from pet product retailers. The whelping box should be large enough for the mother dog to be able to lie comfortably on her side and also to be able to turn around.

The whelping box is not only the "delivery room" where the puppies will be born, it will also be the "nursery" where they will spend the very important first few weeks of their lives. The box needs to be deep enough to keep in a litter of rambunctious American Staffordshire or American pit bull terrier puppies, but the sides should not be so high that the now low-slung mother dog has trouble getting in or out.

Cover the floor of the whelping box with black and white newspaper. Do not use the brightly printed color advertisements or special sections. Always put layers of newspaper in the box so that as the puppies soil the top layer it can be removed, leaving other layers below it. This will make cleaning the box easy and not too upsetting for the mother or the pups.

Place the whelping box in a dry, warm place away from drafts and too many passersby. Your APBT/Amstaff mother dog will need to feel that her babies are safe and she will do much better without the constant distraction of the regular household hubbub. Remember that these are *her* babies. Don't let the newness and cuteness of the newborn puppies cause you and your family to bring even more stress on the mother.

Note: A *very* important specification of the whelping box is a shelf inside it that will help prevent a puppy from being caught and crushed between the side of the box and its mother's body!

Getting Ready for the Birth Day

By building or purchasing a whelping box, you have set into place an action plan for the puppies' arrival. American pit bull terriers/American Staffordshire terriers are generally very good mothers, but you may want to schedule some time off from work in order to be near her, especially if this is her first litter. You can expect her to become restless as the big day nears. Remember to be very gentle

Arranged in front of this whelping box are the "kit" items that you may need. The whelping box itself has a protective shelf that will keep puppies from being accidentally crushed by their mother's body.

and tender with her to let her know that she is still important, regardless of all the changes she is experiencing.

You were the one that decided that this litter of puppies was such a good idea. Although she would have probably gone along with it without your involvement (or even your choice of sires), you should make every allowance for her during this time. Try to spend as much time as you can with her, especially during the last couple of weeks when she has been segregated from any other dogs you may have and has gone on a nonstrenuous schedule.

Visit with your veterinarian and with your experienced APBT/Amstaff breeder friends. There are several books that go into greater depth about your role on whelping day. Now is the time to *know* what to do, not just think that you know, or to pretend that you know! Although many millions of dogs have whelped puppies without assistance, this litter should represent the best of your efforts in obtaining an APBT/Amstaff of excellent quality, giving her a chance to prove her worthiness to become a matron (and perhaps a matriarch) of the breed by contracting for the top available stud dog in terms of temperament, condition, quality, and genetic compatibility. Don't drop the ball now by failing to adequately prepare for the big moment!

Whelping

Under normal conditions, the mother dog will pull away the birth sac and chew through the umbilical cord as each newborn makes its appearance. If she doesn't do this, you may have to assist her (which is the reason for your scissors and the surgical twine).

The mother normally licks each puppy to clean it and will gently nudge it toward her milk-filled teats for its first meal. If you try to help her by toweling off the new youngster and placing him at the "lunch counter," move very

Preparing Your Whelping Kit

Prepare a whelping kit that will include these things (and others that your veterinarian or breeder friends may suggest):

• A heating pad in a temporary-care box for the early arrivals.
• Heavy surgical thread and a pair of sharp scissors for cutting and tying off the umbilical cords.
• Clean, soft, unscented, absorbent toweling with which to gently dry off the little, newborn Amstaffs or American pit bull terriers.
• A list of important phone numbers including your veterinarian's office, home, or beeper number (in case of an emergency) and your experienced APBT/Amstaff mentor's (who may even sit in with you if it is okay with the mother APBT/Amstaff).
• You might also want a portable phone nearby so that you can describe a situation, but be sure that it won't ring during whelping and disturb your mother dog!
• A pre-set agreement with the other members of your family to stay away from where the whelping box is until the births are complete.
• A notepad and something to write with to jot down observations about which puppy was born first and other information that you may want to remember. Some breeders have very light fabric rings of elastic of different colors that can be placed on each puppy for identification.

slowly and deliberately. Speak softly to the mother and don't do anything to upset her or to divert her attention from the next puppy to be born.

After each puppy is born, some afterbirth should be expelled, which the mother will usually eat. If, after all the puppies are born, you have reason to believe that there may still be some afterbirth that has not been expelled, call your veterinarian.

There may be quite some time between the birth of the first puppy and the birth of the last one to be born. You can place the earlier pups in your heated (not hot), towel-lined box. This will make certain that the older puppies aren't chilled as their younger siblings are being born.

Caring for the New Puppies

You have been there to welcome these puppies and helped their mother get them off to a good start. Now your part of this job is really just beginning! Many things have to be done to give these helpless babies the best possible chance at becoming what they have been carefully bred to be.

The area where the puppies begin their lives should be kept at a warm, consistent temperature between 80 and 85°F (26.7–29.4°C). Young puppies simply cannot endure large fluctuations in temperature. Their mother will do her best to keep them warm, but she has a short, tight coat that doesn't have much insulation ability to share with her babies. Make certain that you keep the mother and offspring within a good temperature range.

As the puppies mature, they will be less vulnerable to temperature extremes. You may then use an external heating source, a light or a small heater. Make certain that this source is not too close to the puppies or within their inquisitive reach. Puppy-proofing starts all over again, right here and right now. Make certain that the area around the whelping box is free of dangers for the adventurous pup that may somehow get out of the whelping box!

Your mother American pit bull terrier or Amstaff will generally do an excellent job in caring for her babes during their first weeks of life. She will feed them, clean them, and clean up after

Now that you have bred a litter of puppies, you have the task of finding the best possible homes for them.

them. Even before their eyes have opened, the puppies have begun to learn things from their mother. She will be the center of their limited, little universe and usually will provide most of the care they will need.

If she dies, has too many puppies to care for, or for any reason can't give them what they need, you become the surrogate mother! You will have to feed them with a veterinarian-approved mother's milk replacer. That job is not as simple or as much fun as it sounds. Hungry little terriers will need to be fed about every four hours during the first weeks of their lives. That is every four hours *without fail.* The litter will serve as a feeding timer for you. If you are even a little late, their loud whimpers will serve to spur you into action! One very positive result of this hand-feeding experience is the unique bonding that will take place between you and your APBT/Amstaff foster children.

When the pups are around six weeks old, they will need their first temporary shots. Your veterinarian can also do their initial exams and check them for worms at this time. Although they are still too young to leave home and their mama, they are beginning to grow rapidly. Your next jobs are nearly at hand.

Weaning the puppies at the appropriate time is a crucial stage in their development. This can be assisted by gradually shifting them from a diet of mother's milk exclusively to an increasing taste for puppy food. Start with a top-quality dry puppy mixture. Introduce the little ones to this new food by moistening bits of it and letting them lick the intriguing new taste off your fingers. Their first actual sampling of the food will need to be damp but not soggy.

As the puppies learn to eat the new food, gradually cut back on the moisture, but make sure that they have drinking water nearby. Use a flat-bottomed pan to feed these now quite active youngsters. This will keep them from upsetting the pan and the cleanliness of the whelping box. Make certain that the food and water bowls are thoroughly cleaned each day. The cleaner their environment, the better chance these pups will have!

Note: Adult dogs can sometimes harbor illnesses that can strike vulnerable puppies. It is very important that these puppies *not* have contact with dogs other than their mother and littermates until after they have received their vaccinations. It is also important that they not be exposed to fecal material, toys, and living areas of other adult dogs until they have received the last of their immunizations at 16 to 18 weeks. Because some Amstaff/APBT breeders maintain that their breeds are harder to immunize than some others, this is especially good advice!

Socialization

As stated earlier, it is very important that puppies, especially American pit bull terrier puppies and American Staffordshire puppies, get early and thorough socialization. Introduce them to humans other than their family or their veterinarian. Usually puppies make friends with strangers quickly, but never underestimate the effect that this early socialization will have on these pups for the rest of their lives!

Socialization gives American pit bull terrier and American Staffordshire terrier puppies a chance to meet other humans, come to like them, and learn not to fear them.

Good Homes for the Puppies

The position you were in when you were seeking your first American pit bull terrier or American Staffordshire terrier is now reversed! You are the breeder. You are the one concerned about finding the best possible homes for your puppies. You will have to provide guarantees and pedigrees.

The best advice for you as a new breeder with puppies to place is to remember what you went through

Socializing Your Puppies

• Pick out as many different types of people as you can. For example, don't neglect different ethnic groups, people in wheelchairs, small children and babies, and older people. When these puppies leave your home with their new owners, you want them to be as comfortable in as many human-canine situations as possible.
• Give each puppy some individual attention every day. You might take each puppy with you at a different time to meet other people, to a shopping mall, to places where the sights, sounds, and smells will all be new.
• Be gentle with the little ones. Rough play with these little terriers, as tough as they already may be, is inappropriate and may convey some wrong messages.
• Treat each puppy as an individual. Not all puppies will have the same personality. Try to recognize each youngster's innate differences and key your socialization for each puppy individually, not for the entire litter as a group.
• Be consistent with them. It is never too early to begin building on the lessons their mother has taught them.

searching for a pup. Use your breed-mentor to help you. Set definite standards for what you will accept as a future for each puppy. Avoid the temptation to give the show-quality puppies (if you are fortunate enough to have any in your first litter) good care while letting the potential pets slide by. When you decided to bring this litter into the world, you made a commitment to lifelong responsibility for each of the puppies you allowed to be born. Live up to it now!

Useful Addresses and Literature

A healthy, well-bred, well-socialized American pit bull terrier or American Stafforshire terrier puppy headed to a home where it will receive lots of love and good care is the best end product of any dog-breeding activity!

International Kennel Clubs and Breed Clubs

Staffordshire Terrier Club of America*
Richard Pascoe, M.D.
785 Valley View Road
Forney, Texas 75126

American Kennel Club
51 Madison Avenue
New York, New York 10038

Canadian Kennel Club
89 Skyway Avenue
Etobicoke, Ontario
Canada M9W 6R4

United Kennel Club, Inc.
100 East Kilgore Road
Kalamazoo, Michigan 49001

Breeder Referral Organization

Staffordshire Terrier Club of America
    Breeder Referral*
Sharon Gregory, Chairperson
1431 New York Avenue
Columbus, New Jersey 08022

Books

Alderton, David. *The Dog Care Manual.* Hauppauge, New York: Barron's Educational Series, Inc., 1986.

Baer, Ted. *Communicating with Your Dog.* Hauppauge, New York: Barron's Educational Series, Inc., 1989.

Klever, Ulrich. *The Complete Book of Dog Care.* Hauppauge, New York: Barron's Educational Series, Inc., 1990.

Ullman, Hans. *The New Dog Handbook.* Hauppauge, New York: Barron's Educational Series, Inc., 1984.

Wrede, Barbara. *Civilizing Your Puppy.* Hauppauge, New York: Barron's Educational Series, Inc., 1992.

* This address may change with the election of new club officers. The current listing can be obtained by contacting the American Kennel Club.

Index

Accidents, 82
Addresses, 110
Afterbirth, 107
Air travel, 47
Allergies, 87
Alpha dog, 66
American Boarding Kennel
    Association, 49, 110
American bulldog, 7
American Kennel Club (AKC),
    6, 12, 14, 35, 110
American Kennel Club (AKC)
    Standard, 16
American pit bull terrier (name),
    14
American Staffordshire terrier
    (name), 14
Amino acids, 58
Anal sac impaction, 86
Anestrus, 104
Antifreeze, 94

Balanced diet, 57
Bennett, C. Z., 14
Birth, 106
Bleeding, 93
Bloat (gastric torsion), 86
Blue Paul (Blue Poll), 13
Boarding, 48
Books, 110
Bordetella, 85
Bowls, 41
Boston terrier, 11
Boxer, 7
Breeding, 99–109
Brucellosis, 103
Brushes, 41
Bull-and-terrier breeds, 11
Bulldog, 10
    American, 7
Bull mastiff, 11
Bull terrier, 11
    Staffordshire, 12

Canadian Kennel Club, 110
Canine hip dysplasia, 36, 86
Canned dog food, 62
Car travel, 46
Carbohydrates, 58
Carrier, 47
Changing food, 61
Chews, 95
Children, 19, 20
Coat, 41, 45, 87
Collar, 74, 75
Combs, 41, 46
"Come" command, 79
Commands, 75–80
Coronavirus, 85
Crate training, 53, 72

Dalmatian, 11
Dam, 101
Deer tick, 90
Demodectic mange, 90
Dental care, 94
Diarrhea, 86
Distemper, 83
Dog biscuits, 63
Dog sign language, 20
Double registration, 32
"Down" command, 78
Dry dog food, 62

Ear mites, 90
Ears, 95
Emergency care, 93
England, 11, 13
English terrier (white), 11
Equipment, 74
Estrous cycle, 104
Estrus, 104
Euthanasia, 98
External parasites, 89
Eyes, 95

Fats, 58

Feeding, 57–63
Feet, 96
Females, 15, 31, 60, 104
Fences, 27, 29, 30, 32, 42
Fighters, 6, 8, 13
Flea-bite allergy, 89
Fleas, 89

Gait, 15, 17, 87
Great Dane, 6
Greyhound, 11
Grooming, 45
Guard dogs, 23

Health certificate, 47
Health records, 35, 83
Heartworms, 89
Heat, 31, 99
Heatstroke, 93
"Heel" comand, 77
Hepatitis, 84
Hinks, James, 11
Hip dysplasia, 36, 86
Homemade diets, 63
Hookworms, 88
Housebreaking, 53, 68, 70
Housing, 42

Immunizations, 82, 108
Inherited conditions, 88
Injuries, 92
Insurance, 32, 37
Internal parasites, 88
Ireland, 13

Lactation, 104
Legs, 15, 17
Leptospirosis, 84
Literature, 110
Lyme disease, 85

Males, 15, 31, 60, 102
Mange, 90

Mastiff, 11
Mating, 104
Medicine, 97
Metestrus, 104
Milk production, 104
Minerals, 58
Mites, 90
Mosquitoes, 89
Muzzle, 92

Nails, 96
Neck, 15, 16
Neutering, 37, 60
Nose, 15, 16
Nutrition, 57

Obedience classes, 80
OFA certification numbers, 36
Old age, 59, 97
"Old Family Red Nose" strain, 13
Ovaries, 104
Ovulation, 104

Pack behavior, 66
Paper training, 69
Parainfluenza, 85
Parasites, 88–91
Parked cars, 93
Parvovirus, 85
Pedigree, 36, 102
Pet-quality dog, 31
Pets, 22, 31
Phosphorus, 58
Picking up a puppy, 43
Poisoning, 93
Praise, 70, 71, 76, 78, 79
Pregnancy, 105
Proestrus, 104
Protein, 58

Puppies, 35, 40
  adjustment, 51–56
  bringing home, 54
  care, 107–109
  feeding, 59
  housebreaking, 68–71
  inoculations, 82
  selecting, 40
  socialization, 50, 109
  training, 64, 67, 73–80
  weaning, 108
  whelping, 106–107
Puppy-proofing, 38–39

Rabies, 83
Red mange, 90
Registration certificate, 35
Relief area, 53, 70
Responsibilities, 30
Rottweillers, 18
Roundworms, 88

Sarcoptic mange, 91
Scabies, 91
Schutzhund, 27
Scotland, 13
Semimoist dog food, 62
Show-quality dog, 31
"Sit" command, 75
Skin problems, 87
Socialization, 50, 109
Spay or neuter agreement, 37
Spaying, 60
Staffordshire bull terrier (name),
  12, 14
Staffybull, 12, 14
"Stay" command, 76
Stretcher, makeshift, 92
Stud dog, 102

Stud fee, 102

Table scraps, 61
Tapeworms, 89
Tartar, 94
Teats, 106
Teeth, 94
Temperature requirements, 107
Terriers, 11
Ticks, 90, 91
Tourniquet, 93
Toys, 41, 51
Tracheobronchitis, 85
Training, 64–80
Travel, 46–48
Treats, 63
Trimming nails, 96

Umbilical cord, 106
United Kennel Club (UKC), 14,
  110
United Kennel Club (UKC)
  Standard, 15
Uterus, 104

Vaccinations, 82, 108
Vaginal discharge, 104
Veterinarian, 81, 92, 98, 106,
  108
Vitamins, 58
Vomiting, 86
Vulva, 104

Water, 58
Weaning, 108
Weight, 61
Whelping, 106, 107
Whimpering, 54
Worms, 88